SOCIAL SITUATION MAPPING

Making Sense of the Social World

Michelle Garcia Winner & Pamela Crooke

Think Social Publishing, Inc.
Santa Clara, California
www.socialthinking.com

Social Situation Mapping: Making Sense of the Social World
Michelle Garcia Winner and Pamela Crooke

Copyright © 2023 Think Social Publishing, Inc.

Previously titled *Social Behavior Mapping* (2019, 2007).

The Social Thinking® Methodology is made up of language-based curricula, frameworks, and strategies. Because our methodology is dynamic, the language we use to teach evolves along with the culture at large combined with the feedback we get directly from our clients and community. This new release includes a new title, new cover, and important content updates to descriptive language to teach basic concepts.

All Rights Reserved except as noted herein.

Outside of the specific use described below, all other reproduction/copying, adaptation, conversion to electronic format, or sharing/distribution of content, through print or electronic means, is not permitted without written permission from Think Social Publishing, Inc. (TSP).

This includes prohibition of any use of any content or materials from this product as part of an adaptation or derivative work you create for posting on a personal or business website, TeachersPayTeachers, YouTube, Pinterest, Facebook, or any other social media or information sharing site in existence now or in the future, whether free or for a fee. Exceptions are made, upon written request, for product reviews, articles, and blogposts.

Think Social Publishing, Inc. (TSP) grants permission to the owner of this book to use and/or adapt content in print or electronic form, only for direct in-classroom/school/home or in-clinic use with your own students/clients/children, and with the primary stakeholders in that individual's life, which includes parents/caregivers and direct service personnel. The copyright for any adaptation of content owned by TSP remains with TSP as a derivative work.

Social Thinking, Superflex, The Unthinkables, The UnthinkaBots, The Thinkables, and We Thinkers! GPS are trademarks belonging to TSP.

Translation of this product can only be done in accordance with our TRANSLATION POLICY found on our intellectual property website page here: https://www.socialthinking.com/intellectual-property.

And, visit our intellectual property page to find detailed TERMS OF USE information and a DECISION-TREE that cover copyright, trademark, and intellectual property topics and questions governing the use of our materials.

ISBN: 978-1-936943-94-4 (print)
ISBN: 978-1-936943-96-8 (ebook)

Think Social Publishing, Inc.
404 Saratoga Avenue, Suite 200
Santa Clara, CA 95050
Tel: (408) 557-8595
Fax: (408) 557-8594

This book was printed and bound in the United States.

TSP is a sole source provider of Social Thinking products in the U.S.

Books may be purchased online at www.socialthinking.com

Recommended Teaching & Learning Pathway
for using Social Situation Mapping

Social Situation Mapping can be used alongside and to support the teachings found in these core books about Social Thinking®

Described in detail in this book

Lessons on how to regulate to navigate within the social world

Many examples of filled out Social Situation Maps

Core concepts explained within Social Situation Mapping are explored in Social Thinking materials for different age groups

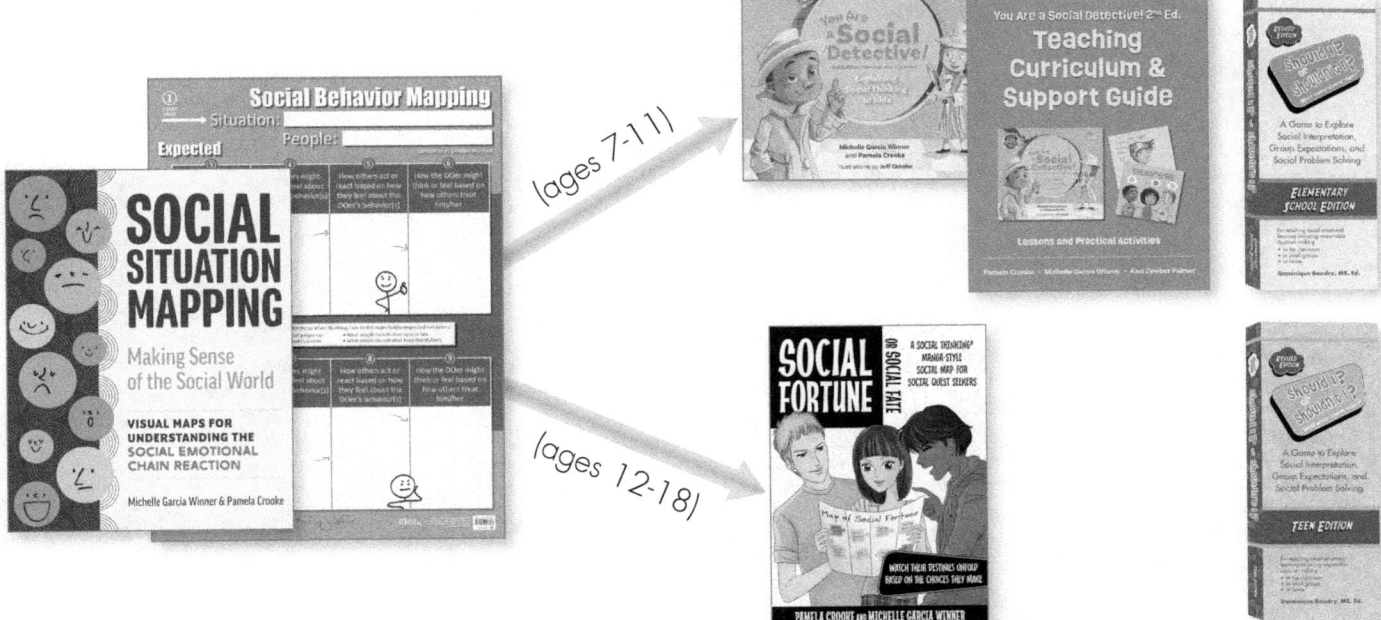

(ages 7-11)

(ages 12-18)

Find these and other books and teaching materials at
www.SocialThinking.com

Contents

Introduction ix

Social Situation Mapping (Template) xviii
Social Situation Mapping (Completed) xix
Social Situation Mapping: 10-Step Visual Guide xx
Adding the 10 Steps to the SSMs in this Book xxi
Social Situation Maps 1

TRANSPORTATION
Riding in the Car with Family 2
Riding in an Airplane 4
Riding on a School Bus with Peers 6
Riding on a Public Bus with Strangers 8

COPING WITH SCHOOL AND HOMEWORK
Eating in the School Cafeteria with Peers 10
Computer or Tablet Activities at School 12
Initiating Play with Others at School 14
Silent Reading in the Classroom with Peers 16
Participating in Art Class with Classmates 18
Free Time in Class 20
Unscheduled or Waiting Time at School 22
Getting Ready and Playing at Recess with Others 24
Standing in Line with Others at School 26
Waiting for the Teacher to Start Class 28
Independent Desk Work in Class 30
Participating in Class Discussions 32
Note-Taking During Class Time 34
Using the Bathroom at School 36

Getting Into a Work Group with Peers in Class..38

Working in a Small Group in Class 40

Preparing to Leave a Class Each Day 42

Time Between Classes with Peers (Adults Not Around).....................................44

Preparing to Go Home from School...46

Thinking About Schoolwork at Home 48

Actual Time Doing Homework...50

Studying at Home (Parents or Caregivers are Home) 52

SOCIAL ACTIVITIES

Sending and Receiving Texts at School..54

Safety Online and on Social Media 56

Visiting Another Person's House 58

Having Visitors when Adults are Home 60

At a School Dance 62

PERSONAL HYGIENE

Flossing at Home...64

Daily Hygiene Routine at Home or when Traveling 66

Using a Public Toilet...68

Using the Urinal in a Public Bathroom 70

AT HOME WITH FAMILY

Mealtime with Family 72

Sharing with Siblings at Home 74

Doing Chores at Home (Parents or Caregivers are Home) 76

Watching TV with Others at Home..78

Needing Help When Others Are Busy 80

Getting Ready for Bed at Home..82

Acknowledgments

Since 1998 many different neurodiverse and neurodivergent individuals, parents, caregivers and professionals have provided valuable insights which have helped to form the basis of Social Situation Maps (formerly Social Behavior Maps) and how they have evolved over time.

Introduction
Social Situation Mapping
What is it? Teaching it with Fidelity

This book and the concepts being taught are best suited for use with individuals age 9 and older. Information is provided at the end of this Introduction to explain how to teach parts of this process to children younger than 9 years old.

Social Situation Mapping (formerly called Social Behavior Mapping) is a social learning teaching framework that is one part of the larger Social Thinking® Methodology. It has been available to the public since 2002. Since that time, the creators of the Social Thinking Methodology have evolved best practices when utilizing Social Situation Maps (SSMs), to encourage that these maps be used constructively to promote social emotional learning, rather than destructively (to place blame and possible punishment on the DOer of the unexpected behavior).

SSMs were initially developed for persons with social learning differences (e.g., autism spectrum levels 1 and 2, ADHD, twice exceptional, etc.) to deconstruct and make sense out of an endless array of abstract social landscapes. However, they are now commonly adopted as part of social emotional learning (SEL) with not only students, but adults from all walks of life, around the globe. This tool provides clarity for how we each impact one another, across an endless array of social contexts. A primary message taught through Social Situation Mapping is that social behavior is not something produced in isolation. Instead any behavior that is perceived by others is a social behavior. All social behavior is interpreted by others and possibly responded to. How one perceives, interprets, and responds to the "DOer's" behavior may have significant impact on the DOer as well as the responder.

Bottom line is this. Through SSMs we are teaching that each context-specific behavior produced by a DOer is likely to influence others' thoughts and feelings, which can then impact how these others react and respond to the DOer in that context. This is then likely to impact, positively or negatively, the DOer's further reaction and response. This process is cyclical, with DOers and responders changing roles quickly, which is why our social behavior is both synergistic and dynamic.

Critical Vocabulary

Social Emotional Chain Reaction
Social Situation Mapping
DOer

The Social Emotional Chain Reaction (SECR) is the basis for Social Situation Mapping. The SECR begins by defining the context, which is both the situation within an environment and what is known about the people in that situation (e.g., teacher, peers, friends, strangers, etc.). The DOer in each SECR is the person(s) who is producing specific expected or unexpected behavior in that context. The people in that context interpret what is happening. This results in thoughts and feelings they might have about the DOer's behavior, which results in these people's specific responses and/or reactions. How the DOer is responded to by others might impact how the DOer then feels and responds in return. If people are responding to a DOer's expected behavior in that context, their response will most likely be positive or neutral. If people are responding to a DOer's unexpected behavior in that context, their response might be more confused, frustrated, or possibly another negative emotion.

We define the contextually based behavior-feelings-reactions sequence as the **Social Emotional Chain Reaction** (SECR), as illustrated below.

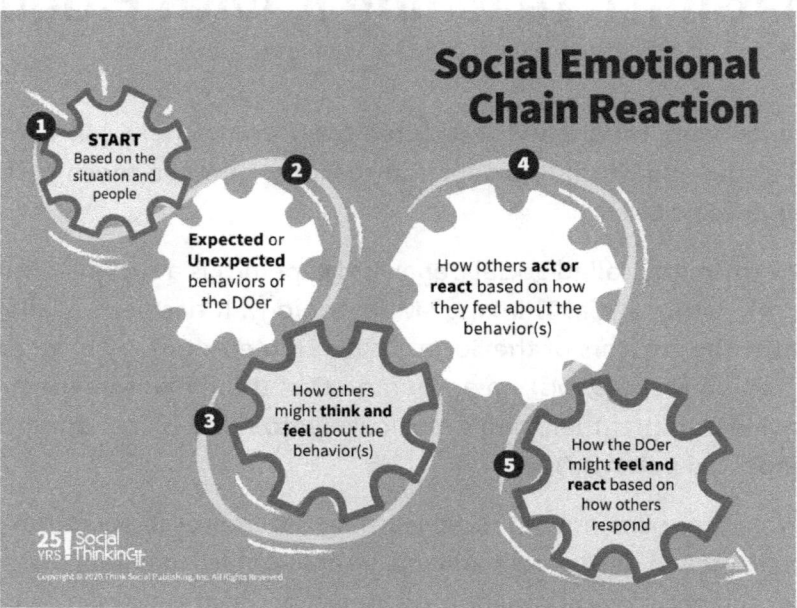

A Social Situation Map is a visual graphic teaching tool that highlights each aspect of the SECR, with the SECR for expected behavior explored separately from the SECR for unexpected behavior in this one teaching framework.

Traditional teachings, even in the world of social emotional learning, often make assumptions about what individuals already understand about how people co-exist and/or interact across an array of social contexts. It is often assumed children and adults understand the Social Emotional Chain Reaction. Teaching tools within the Social Thinking Methodology purposefully avoid these social emotional assumptions by exploring explicitly many of our more implicit contextually based social agreements (hidden rules).

Behaviorally based teaching programs are typically focused on teaching behavior or chains of behaviors without teaching this more complex, abstract social emotional processing embedded in the SECR. When utilizing SSMs to help individuals learn about their own and others' expectations within the SECR, the focus is less on "behaving" and is more about figuring out and learning to participate in the social problem solving that occurs any time we are in the presence of others, or making sense of others' actions and reactions on screen or within graphics or text. This process is an integral part of developing social competencies, which is more than teaching social skills. SSMs are designed to teach SECR to foster social understanding and responsibility we have for each other rather than focus on teaching the precise production specific behaviors with the goal of getting individuals to "behave."

SSMs were designed for use in schools, communities, and homes. The goal is to help students (learners in and outside the classroom) focus on learning about the SECR without having to write much language! For this reason the SSM template consists of several columns where students write in single words or short phrases that best represent the main idea of what they want to convey.

The way we teach Social Situation Mapping has evolved over time in response to how the community utilized our materials. Initially SSMs were developed to 1) teach students how to "read" the contextually based expectations as they learned about the Social Emotional Chain Reaction; and 2) develop awareness of the production and impact of their own personal expected and unexpected behaviors on others.

However, we found that most adult interventionists were solely using SSMs to explain to students the mistakes they were making, and at times punishing them for producing unexpected behaviors because "they knew about the expected side of the map but chose not to do it"! As a result, students were becoming averse to any mention of "expected" and "unexpected" behaviors and they certainly did not want to see an SSM!

We now have better ways of explaining how to move through the social learning process with the goal of developing improved social competencies rather than focus on how an individual is behaving. This goes beyond teaching "good social skills" or "expected/unexpected behavior." It involves teaching our students through four steps: 1) social attention; 2) social interpretation; 3) social problem solving to make a decision about… 4) how to socially respond based on our personal social goals. (This four-step process is the cornerstone of our Social Competency Model, which is explained in detail in our free online article, "The Expanded Social Thinking–Social Competency Model (ST-SCM)" (Winner & Crooke, 2022), available at socialthinking.com.

Rather than use SSMs to draw attention to individuals' own behavior as the first step and as a means for teaching behavior change, we have found it far more effective to utilize SSMs to increase awareness of the hidden expectations tied to specific contexts through the lens of the social observer, rather than the interactive participant. After all, most of us spend far more time observing and interpreting others' intentions, actions and reactions, than actually interacting with others. Over the last 18 years of using SSMs, we have learned that taking time to teach individuals to figure out their own social expectations for others lays the foundation for them to gradually learn more about their own social self-regulation as part of this larger process of social responsibility within specific contexts.

Using the SSM to Explore the SECR: Avoid Focusing on the Student as the DOer

As noted above, it's extremely important that when we introduce SSMs, our goal is that individuals become familiar with the Social Emotional Chain Reaction by **starting as observers of the context** (e.g., Social Detective or Social Spy). We actively avoid them being the "DOer" of behaviors (whether they are expected or unexpected) and instead put them in the role of only being the observer who is actively engaging their social attention and social interpretation as they establish their social expectations for the people in this context. When individuals are not at risk for being called out or corrected for their unexpected behavior, they can focus on being objective observers to help them learn about the SECR process for both expected and unexpected behaviors.

Learning objectives:

1. Identify the context.
    a. Situation = Place + What's happening?
    b. Identify what is known about the people in the situation.

2. Identify the *unexpected behaviors* a DOer(s) may produce in this context.

3. Based on the unexpected behavior, determine the *hidden expectations*, which are *expected behaviors* the DOer is to produce. To figure out the expected behaviors, provide prosocial alternatives to the unexpected behavior(s) noted in the earlier step.

4. Identify how the other people in this context might feel or think about the DOer's expected versus unexpected behaviors.

5. Based on the the observer's feelings or thoughts about the expected versus the unexpected behaviors, identify how others might react and respond.

6. Identify what the DOer(s) might feel or think about their expected and unexpected behaviors based on how others responded (as indicated in the earlier boxes on the SSM.)

7. Explain how each box on the SECR for expected and unexpected behavior is related to each other by providing examples of how a DOer's behavior impacted information identified in each of the other three columns.

8. Sum it up by "drawing the map" for the expected and/or unexpected SECR, showing the behavior-thoughts/feelings-reaction connection. Details on how to do this are explained below.

See a sample of a completed SSM and the SSM template at the end of the Introduction.

Instructions

Every SSM has three sections, organized in a way that helps guide our discussions:

1. The Situation and the People
2. The SECR for Expected Behaviors (first row of boxes)
3. The SECR for Unexpected Behaviors (second row of boxes)

(Note there are numbers associated with each section on the SSM. Those numbers align with the 10 steps completed as described below.)

These later two sections each consist of four columns that organize thinking through the SECR:

1. Behavior(s) (expected or unexpected) given the context (situation and people)
2. How others might feel (or think) about the behavior(s)
3. How others might act or react based on how they feel (or think)
4. How the DOer might feel (or think) based on how others respond

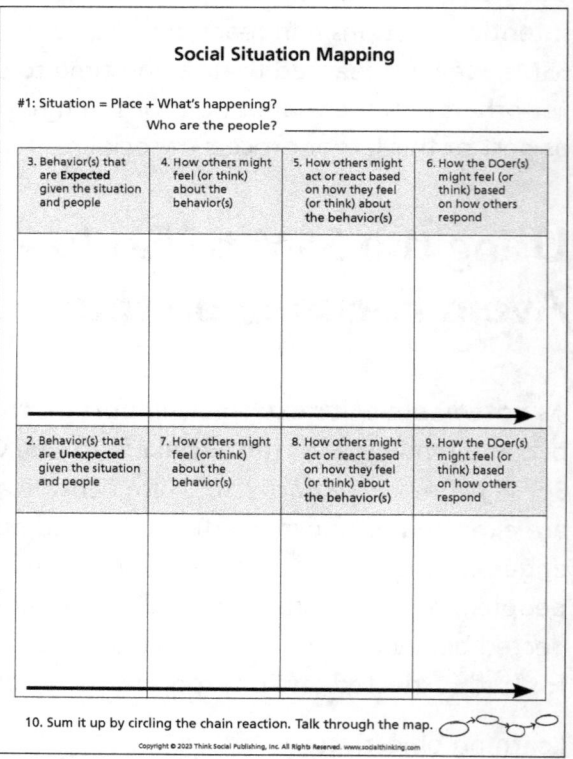

Use the following 10 steps as a guide in introducing SSMs. These 10 steps are also summarized in a chart at the end of this introduction.

STEP 1: IDENTIFY THE CONTEXT

Have students note the situation and the people in the situation at the top of the map.

Defining the Situation. The situation is different from the environment. A teacher may be teaching in a classroom (environment), but the classroom has many different situations (e.g., getting ready to learn, teaching/talking time, class discussion time, individual work time, group work time, standing in line, etc.). Virtually every environment has an array of situations. The playground has a vast array of situations, as does our dining rooms at home, the school library may have a lecture going on, quiet reading time, group discussion time, etc.

It is important to note that a situation is never a behavior! If a person is yelling, swearing, getting up from their desk, etc. these are all behaviors that are to be noted in box 2 and not as the Situation!

It takes practice to socially attend and interpret within an environment to "read the situation" accurately.

An important part of this includes defining the people in a situation to help us figure out the hidden expectations. People in a situation may be friends, classmates, unknown peers, teachers, family members, principal, substitute teacher, etc. For example, a 12-year-old telling a disgusting joke to another 12-year-old makes them both laugh, but if a teacher is present the joke may fall flat or get the child in trouble.

This type of interpretation will always be important when trying to navigate any social scenario, whether using an SSM or not!

Being able to attend to and interpret context directly supports core academic curriculum. Whether students are engaged in reading comprehension of fiction, studying history or social studies, it is important for students to be able to decipher the context (situation and people) for them to comprehend what is happening in the academic texts presented to them. The social mind guides us to interpret information for academic success!

STEP 2: IDENTIFY THE UNEXPECTED BEHAVIORS IN THAT CONTEXT

This is the only counterintuitive step in the process of teaching individuals to use SSMs and for this reason, we have added numbers to our SSMs that represent the sequence of steps to go through in completing a map.

Look at the blank map and you will see that #1 is identifying the situation and people and #2 is in the lower left-hand box: "Behaviors that are Unexpected Given the Situation and People." The reason students are asked to fill out the section related to the Unexpected Behaviors first is that the human brain tends to actively notice unexpected behaviors as it takes contextually based expected behaviors for granted. Furthermore, exploring these behaviors helps students figure out the desired expected behaviors to replace these specific unexpected behaviors!

Have students write in two to four unexpected behaviors they observe or can imagine happening in that specific context.

STEP 3: IDENTIFY THE EXPECTED BEHAVIORS IN THAT CONTEXT

Now jump up to #3, the box directly above Unexpected Behaviors labeled "Behaviors that are expected given the situation and people." Have students review the unexpected behaviors they wrote in box 2 and now have them figure out the expected form of these unexpected behaviors. See the filled in SSM at the end of this introduction for examples of expected behaviors written in box 3, based on the unexpected behaviors documented in box 2.

You may choose to include a couple of additional expected behaviors when compared to the list of unexpected behaviors. For example, if a student is blurting out an answer in class (unexpected behavior in box 2), the expected behaviors noted in box 3 may include: 1) Think with eyes to notice who is talking to whom; 2) Raise your hand; and 3) Hold a thought in your head until called on.

STEPS 4-9: COMPLETING THE SECR FOR EXPECTED THEN UNEXPECTED BEHAVIORS

Once box 3 is completed, move from left to right filling out boxes 4, 5, and 6 to compete the Expected SECR. Next go down to the Unexpected SECR and complete boxes 7, 8, and 9.

Notice that the title language describing each of these later three boxes is exactly the same for both Expected and Unexpected SECRs. The words written in each of these three boxes should reflect general emotions and reactions that are experienced and demonstrated based on all the behaviors listed in boxes 2 and 3. Hence, any word written in these boxes could relate to most any behavior noted there.

Completing Boxes 4 and 7 (Others' feelings or thoughts)

Boxes 4 and 7 are about other people's feelings (or thoughts) as they pertain to the DOer's behavior. In these boxes the student should write down feelings (or thoughts) expected by people observing the DOer(s). These are usually single words. The words tend to represent positive feelings (or thoughts) when on the Expected SECR and confused or negative feelings (or thoughts) when on the Unexpected SECR. It is often helpful to have a feelings word bank available to help identify feeling words that are relevant for the context.

Completing Boxes 5 and 8 (How others may react and respond)

We encourage you to have individuals document others' reactions based on the three questions that follow:

1. How did the other person's face or body look (e.g., calm face, happy face, confused face, tight body, relaxed body)?

2. What was the other person's tone of voice (e.g., gentle, angry, loud, calm, etc.)?

3. What did the other person say or do (e.g., gave a compliment, nodded positively, sent to principal's office, etc.)?

Completing Boxes 6 and 9 (How the DOer may think or feel)

In these two boxes students can imagine how they may feel, think, react and respond based on how others responded to the DOer in boxes 5 and 8. They can write in this information or ask for help, if they are not sure.

STEP 10 IS UNIQUE

Once all boxes are completed, technically the SSM is complete and the hidden expectations as well as the SECR for both the Expected and Unexpected Behaviors in that situation are revealed. Step 10 guides students to recognize the "map" when using the Social Situation Map.

In the 10th step, after completing their SSM, we ask a student to observe the situation again and then select one word in each of the 4 columns to ultimately represent a specific a pathway through which they may talk about what happened in a specific context. For each column, the student selects the word that best represents the thought, feeling, or action or reaction they observed in that stage and circles it. After circling the 4 words (1 in each column, the student will connect each circle with a line, and the map goes from left to right to reveal a specific SECR! (A finished example can be found on page xix.)

TEACHING INDIVIDUALS HOW TO USE SSMS IN A CONSISTENT FORMAT

At the end of the Introduction we present a 10-Step Visual Guide. This is a review of the fidelity teaching pathway when guiding your students to complete their own social observations using the SSM as they learn about the Social Emotional Chain Reaction across different contexts.

TALKING IT THROUGH THE SSM

"Talking it through the map" refers to verbally explaining how we impact each other, without the use of the SSM visual support/template. This can be successfully done at times, only after individuals are very familiar with the SSM template, the progression through the SECR, and have utilized SSMs to figure out the hidden expectations across a range of situations.

How to Use SSMs to Teach SECR Across Academic Subjects

The Social Thinking Methodology is not just about helping students learn to observe and notice how individuals self-regulate social behavior in context. It extends much further. It demonstrates that the social mind is quite active when students need to interpret and respond to educational expectations within the core curriculum. This social-academic connection is explained in the ILAUGH Model of Social Cognition in more detail. (Learn more about the ILAUGH Model in our *Social Thinking® Frameworks Collection, Core Practical Frameworks Set 1*; in a free article on our website "Understanding Core Social Thinking

Needs: The ILAUGH Model"; and in our four module eLearning series: *The ILAUGH Model: Exploring Social Thinking & the Social-Academic Connection*.)

To follow are some examples of using SSMs to highlight the human experience across various curricula.

LITERATURE

When exploring how characters think and feel about each other in a novel, develop an SSM to analyze how one character's behavior (expected/unexpected) influenced the thoughts, feelings, and related responses of other characters.

HISTORY

When teaching history, use an SSM to highlight how the behavior of a country's leader impacted the thoughts, feelings, and related reactions or responses of leadership in another country (whether allies or enemies).

SOCIAL STUDIES

When exploring how people in different societies work together, create different SSMs to compare and contrast possible expected/unexpected behaviors when greeting others within a culture (on a single map) and across cultures (compare and contrast SSMs representing different cultures). For instance, the use of gestures and eye-contact varies widely from culture to culture. If you use direct eye contact to greet an American elder of Western European Descent, the elder has fine to good feelings and will likely treat you with respect. However, this same type of greeting would offend those of Japanese or Native American descent. Have students research greetings in difficult cultures and do separate maps for each culture. After the maps are completed, have students discuss why it is important to be aware of cultural sensitivity.

PE

When teaching students how to handle team competition in PE, create an SSM so students can explore what it means to be a good sport (expected behaviors and the related SECR) versus a poor loser (unexpected behaviors and the related SECR).

GROUP WORK

When encouraging peer-group work in science labs or any type of group project, have students create an SSM to explore the expected/unexpected behaviors when engaged in group work. Have the team then complete the rest of the boxes on the SSM to have them study how they impact each other positively or negatively as they work together.

Suggestions for Teaching the SECR to Children Younger Than Age Nine

This book and the concepts being taught are best suited for use with individuals age 9 and older. Developmentally children need to first acquire core thinking and processing abilities that facilitate their ability to work through SSMs and consider the thoughts and feelings of others. These include joint attention, perspective taking, executive functioning skills, seeing the big picture (gestalt) and central coherence (understanding how individual details form a conceptual whole). If you are working with children younger than 9 or children with learning and/or developmental differences in any of these areas, please adapt the way you teach.

1. Begin by teaching there are expected and unexpected behaviors based on the situation and the people. (Find lessons for doing this in these Social Thinking titles: *We Thinkers!* Volumes 1 & 2 for ages 4-7; *You Are a Social Detective!* 2nd Ed. for ages 5+; *Think Social!* for ages 4+.)

2. Next teach that how the DOer behaves affects how others think and feel.

3. Only add the last two columns of the SECR (others' responses and DOer's reaction) if you feel your students are able to process and respond to the first points of teaching.

Learn More About the Social Situation Mapping Teaching Framework

- Social Behavior (Situation) Mapping poster-size templates can be hung on a classroom or home wall and actively used as a visual support when discussing any part of the Social Emotional Chain Reaction. The template is available for purchase at www.socialthinking.com.

- Handout-size Social Behavior (Situation) Mapping and Social Emotional Chain Reaction visuals are included in our *Social Thinking Frameworks Collection* that includes 26 visual teaching scaffolds for social learning and self-regulation strategies. Use this collection at home, in a clinic, or at a school in one-on-one settings, in small groups, or for display in classrooms for larger discussions.

We are currently updating the "Social Behavior Mapping" framework name to "Social Situation Mapping" as these products come up for reprint. While these products use the previous term in the title, they include our most recent teaching. These products feature the 10-step Social Behavior (Situation) Map.

On the next few pages, we include the 10-step Social Situation Map template as well as a filled in version. These SSMs include both expected and unexpected behaviors in one map. We also include a 10-step visual guide that explains how to teach this version. The final page of this section shows how to use the maps in this book to create a full 10-step Social Situation Map, if desired.

Social Situation Mapping

#1: Situation = Place + What's happening? _____

Who are the people? _____

3. Behavior(s) that are **Expected** given the situation and people	4. How others might feel (or think) about the behavior(s)	5. How others might act or react based on how they feel (or think) about the behavior(s)	6. How the DOer(s) might feel (or think) based on how others respond
2. Behavior(s) that are **Unexpected** given the situation and people	7. How others might feel (or think) about the behavior(s)	8. How others might act or react based on how they feel (or think) about the behavior(s)	9. How the DOer(s) might feel (or think) based on how others respond

10. Sum it up by circling the chain reaction. Talk through the map.

Copyright © 2023 Think Social Publishing, Inc. All Rights Reserved. www.socialthinking.com

Social Situation Mapping

#1: Situation = Place + What's happening? <u>Listening to the teacher talk</u>

Who are the people? <u>Classroom peers</u>

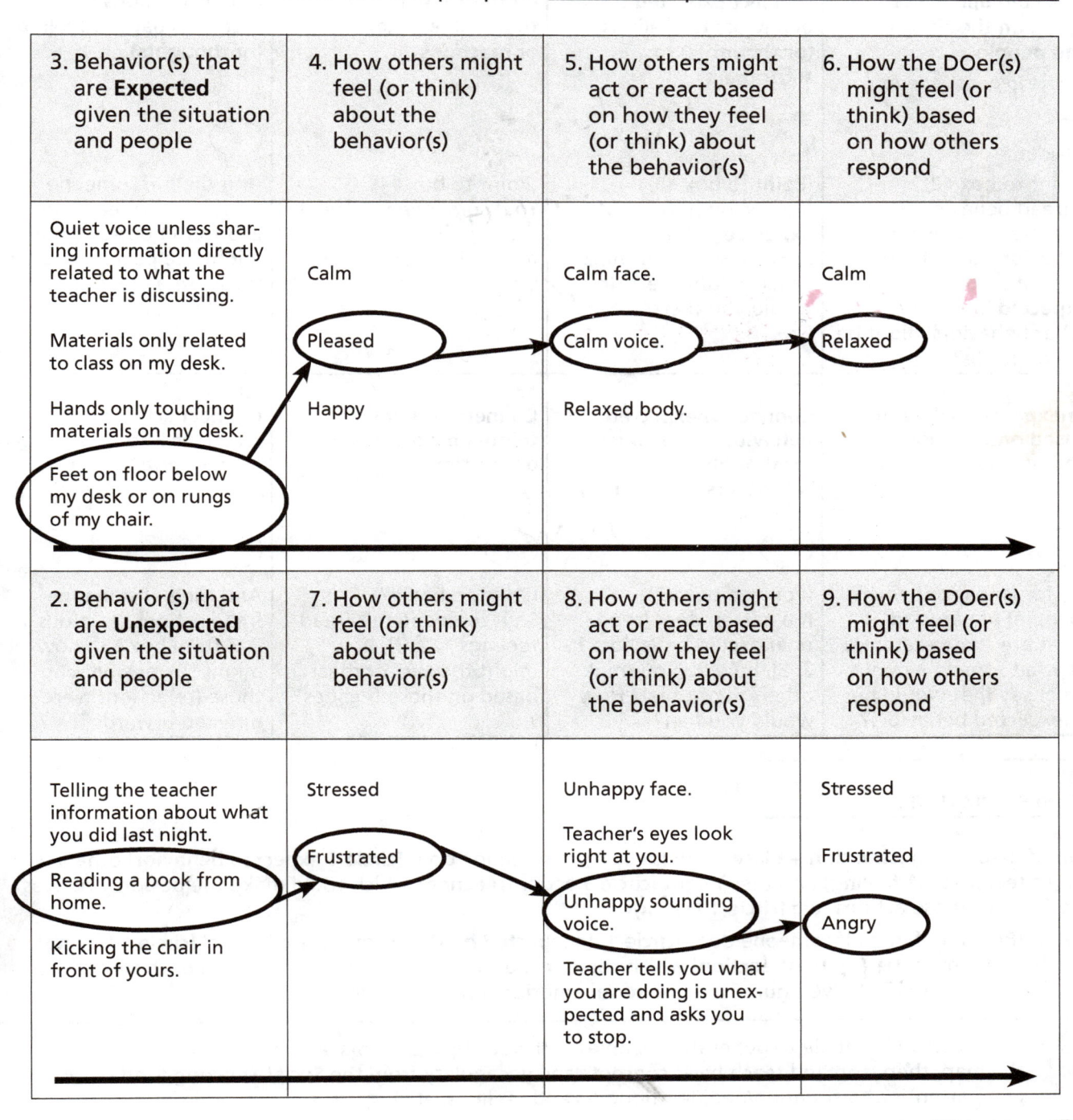

3. Behavior(s) that are **Expected** given the situation and people	4. How others might feel (or think) about the behavior(s)	5. How others might act or react based on how they feel (or think) about the behavior(s)	6. How the DOer(s) might feel (or think) based on how others respond
Quiet voice unless sharing information directly related to what the teacher is discussing. Materials only related to class on my desk. Hands only touching materials on my desk. (Feet on floor below my desk or on rungs of my chair.)	Calm (Pleased) Happy	Calm face. (Calm voice.) Relaxed body.	Calm (Relaxed)

2. Behavior(s) that are **Unexpected** given the situation and people	7. How others might feel (or think) about the behavior(s)	8. How others might act or react based on how they feel (or think) about the behavior(s)	9. How the DOer(s) might feel (or think) based on how others respond
Telling the teacher information about what you did last night. (Reading a book from home.) Kicking the chair in front of yours.	Stressed (Frustrated)	Unhappy face. Teacher's eyes look right at you. (Unhappy sounding voice.) Teacher tells you what you are doing is unexpected and asks you to stop.	Stressed Frustrated (Angry)

10. Sum it up by circling the chain reaction. Talk through the map.

Copyright © 2023 Think Social Publishing, Inc. All Rights Reserved. www.socialthinking.com

Social Situation Mapping: 10-Step Visual Guide

 = Tips for what to say

PRIME & EXPOSE   This guide shows how what we say and do affects others and how they respond.

#1 Define Situation, Place & People	Think about the situation. Consider where + who + what is happening. Go to #2.

#3 Expected behaviors* based on the situation and people *Write in positive terms*	#4 Connect Expected behaviors to feelings (or thoughts) to self/others	#5 Connect feelings to possible actions or reactions	#6 Connect actions or reactions back to feelings (or thoughts)
(Point to box #2) If [read behaviors 1, 2, 3] are **unexpected** behaviors, then the opposite would be **expected** behaviors. What behaviors might be the opposite?	(Point to box #3) If a person [read **expected** behaviors 1, 2, 3], how do you think others might feel? How would you feel?	(Point to box #4) So if someone felt [read feelings 1, 2, 3], how might they act or react based on those feelings?	And then, if someone [read actions/reactions 1, 2, 3 from box #5], how might the person who those (re)actions were directed towards feel?
#2 Unexpected behaviors based on situation and people	**#7 Connect Unexpected behaviors to feelings (or thoughts) to self/others**	**#8 Connect feelings to possible actions or reactions**	**#9 Connect actions or reactions back to feelings (or thoughts)**
So, for [situation] when [people] are around, what are some examples of what someone might do or say that would be unexpected behaviors?	(Point to box #2) If a person does [read **unexpected** behaviors 1, 2, 3], how do you think others might feel? How would you feel?	(Point to box #7) So if someone felt [read feelings 1, 2, 3], how might they act or react based on those feelings?	And then, if someone [read actions/reactions 1, 2, 3 from box #8], how might the person who those (re)actions were directed towards feel?

#10 Circle & SUM IT UP!

Top of map: So, in **[situation + place]** with **[people]**, if someone does **[circle 1 expected behavior]** others might feel **[circle 1 feeling]** and they might **[circle 1 action/reaction]** which could make the person who was the focus of those actions feel **[circle 1 feeling]**.

BUT... (Bottom of map) If someone does **[circle 1 unexpected behavior]** others might feel **[circle 1 feeling]** and they might **[circle 1 action/reaction]** which could make the person who was the focus of those actions feel **[circle 1 feeling]**. You've figured out the social emotional chain reaction!

 If the person is unable to generate examples with your tips, prompts, and examples on any step of the map, then stop and teach basic concepts and vocabulary from the Social Thinking Methodology (e.g., attention to situation/people, thoughts and feelings, etc.).

REMINDER: Teach through the perspective of the observer first.

Copyright © 2023 Think Social Publishing, Inc. All Rights Reserved.

Adding the 10 Steps to the SSMs in this Book

In adapting the filled in maps that follow to incorporate the 10 steps, use these simple instructions.

1. Write in the numbers 1-9 in the appropriate boxes.
2. Remember to discuss that the situation (Step 1) includes place, what's happening, and people.
3. Work through each step in the map as outlined previously. You will only be choosing a few examples in each box to discuss.
4. Step 10 can be written in at the bottom of map, or discussed verbally.

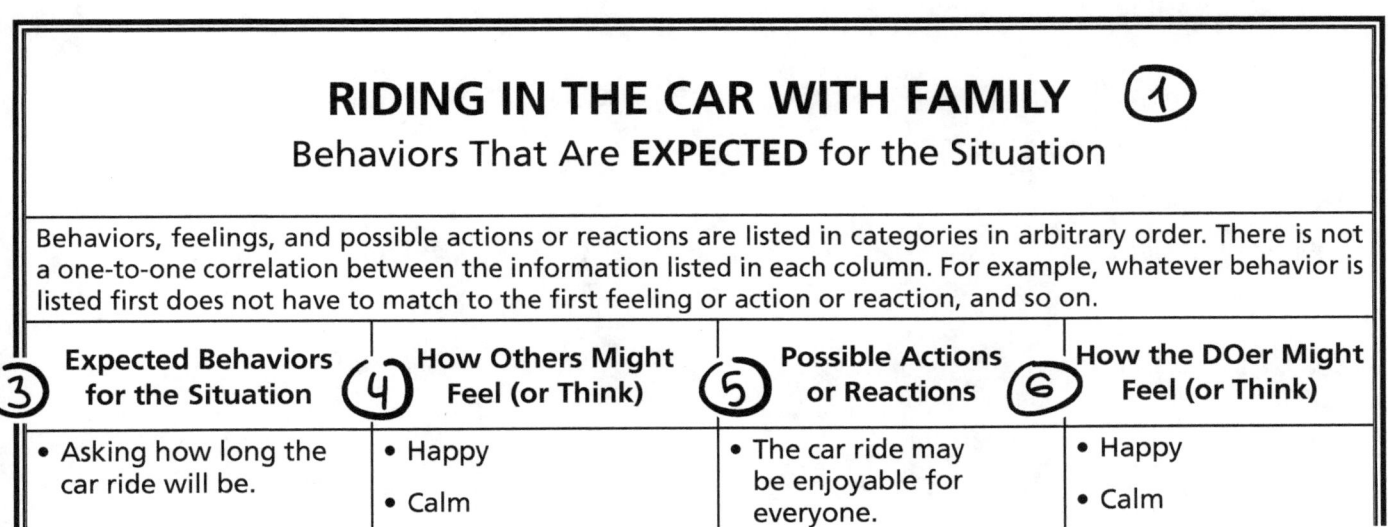

xxi

Social Situation Maps

Visual Maps for Understanding the Social Emotional Chain Reaction

The following pages contain functional examples of SSMs to photocopy and use with children, students, or clients. They cover a wide range of situations at home, school, and in the community and include possible examples of expected and unexpected behaviors you might see in a completed SSM. We do this so you can see the potential in using these maps.

We've enlarged each map by having the Expected and Unexpected examples on separate pages, as well as leaving room for the learner to write in their own ideas after the blank bullets.

RIDING IN THE CAR WITH FAMILY
Behaviors That Are **EXPECTED** for the Situation

Behaviors, feelings, and possible actions or reactions are listed in categories in arbitrary order. There is not a one-to-one correlation between the information listed in each column. For example, whatever behavior is listed first does not have to match to the first feeling or action or reaction, and so on.

Expected Behaviors for the Situation	How Others Might Feel (or Think)	Possible Actions or Reactions	How the DOer Might Feel (or Think)
• Asking how long the car ride will be. • Bringing entertaining things to do for a long car ride. • Going to the bathroom before leaving. • Only touching your books, electronics, toys, or seat with your hands or feet. • Talking calmly to the driver and waiting your turn to talk. • Compromising on the music selection. • •	• Happy • Calm • Relaxed • Appreciated → • •	• The car ride may be enjoyable for everyone. • The driver may be able to better concentrate on driving. • Other people notice how prepared everyone was for the trip. • The driver may feel safer. → • •	• Happy • Calm • Fine with traveling • •

RIDING IN THE CAR WITH FAMILY
Behaviors That Are **UNEXPECTED** for the Situation

Behaviors, feelings, and possible actions or reactions are listed in categories in arbitrary order. There is not a one-to-one correlation between the information listed in each column. For example, whatever behavior is listed first does not have to match to the first feeling or action or reaction, and so on.

Unexpected Behaviors for the Situation	How Others Might Feel (or Think)	Possible Actions or Reactions	How the DOer Might Feel (or Think)
• Refusing to go to the bathroom before a car ride. • Asking over and over again how long the drive is going to be. • Invading other people's personal space or touching their stuff without asking. • Interrupting or scaring the driver. • Turning the music up loud without asking. • Not bringing anything to do in the car. • •	• Confused • Stressed • Annoyed • Anxious • Unhappy • Irritated • Frustrated → • •	• Other people in the car may notice and feel confused. • The driver may have trouble concentrating on driving. • Other people may not think the DOer is thinking about them. • The car ride may be unpleasant. → • •	• Unhappy • Frustrated • Confused • Stressed • Annoyed • •

RIDING IN AN AIRPLANE
Behaviors That Are **EXPECTED** for the Situation

Behaviors, feelings, and possible actions or reactions are listed in categories in arbitrary order. There is not a one-to-one correlation between the information listed in each column. For example, whatever behavior is listed first does not have to match to the first feeling or action or reaction, and so on.

Expected Behaviors for the Situation	How Others Might Feel (or Think)	Possible Actions or Reactions	How the DOer Might Feel (or Think)
• Sitting in assigned seat unless asked to move by flight attendant. • Saying "Excuse me" to get out and go to the bathroom unless sitting in aisle seat. • Putting small bags under the seat in front. • Waiting in line to enter and exit the plane. • Using fidgets, headphones, or other tools to help with sensory needs. • • •	• Calm • Happy • Relaxed • Safe → • •	• Others might notice and make positive comments. • Everyone may enjoy the flight. • Fellow passengers may think the DOer is being considerate. • The DOer might feel proud they understand what to do and how to advocate for their needs on a flight. → • •	• Proud • Excited • Happy to be traveling • Calm • •

RIDING IN AN AIRPLANE
Behaviors That Are **UNEXPECTED** for the Situation

Behaviors, feelings, and possible actions or reactions are listed in categories in arbitrary order. There is not a one-to-one correlation between the information listed in each column. For example, whatever behavior is listed first does not have to match to the first feeling or action or reaction, and so on.

Unexpected Behaviors for the Situation	How Others Might Feel (or Think)	Possible Actions or Reactions	How the DOer Might Feel (or Think)
• Sitting in a seat that is not assigned. • Touching or leaning on people nearby. • Turning on or using an electronic device without permission from the crew. • Walking the aisles when the "Fasten Seat Belt" light is turned on.	• Confused • Annoyed • Angry • Anxious • Scared • Uncomfortable • Stressed	• People may be confused if a person is walking around or invading their space. • Other passengers may feel unsafe. • Flight attendant or travel partner(s) might get upset. • Others may not be able to rest, read, or work.	• Bad • Disturbed • Confused • Uncomfortable • Sad • Frustrated
•	•	•	•
•	•	•	•

RIDING ON A SCHOOL BUS WITH PEERS
Behaviors That Are **EXPECTED** for the Situation

Behaviors, feelings, and possible actions or reactions are listed in categories in arbitrary order. There is not a one-to-one correlation between the information listed in each column. For example, whatever behavior is listed first does not have to match to the first feeling or action or reaction, and so on.

Expected Behaviors for the Situation	How Others Might Feel (or Think)	Possible Actions or Reactions	How the DOer Might Feel (or Think)
• Finding an open seat quickly. • Sitting next to friends or someone familiar. • Sitting next to a new person if there are no friends on the bus. • Only getting on or off when the bus has come to a complete stop. • Sitting near the driver. • Ducking into a seat alone after acknowledging a friend if overwhelmed.	• Calm • Happy • Relaxed • Safe	• The DOer may feel safe and enjoy their bus ride. • Everyone may get to school on time and safely. • People may have friendly relaxed faces and voices.	• Calm • Pleased • Relaxed • Happy
•	•	•	•
•	•	•	•

RIDING ON A SCHOOL BUS WITH PEERS
Behaviors That Are **UNEXPECTED** for the Situation

Behaviors, feelings, and possible actions or reactions are listed in categories in arbitrary order. There is not a one-to-one correlation between the information listed in each column. For example, whatever behavior is listed first does not have to match to the first feeling or action or reaction, and so on.

Unexpected Behaviors for the Situation	How Others Might Feel (or Think)	Possible Actions or Reactions	How the DOer Might Feel (or Think)
• Completely ignoring friends or familiar peers. • Wandering up and down the aisle when the bus is moving. • Kicking a seat nearby. • Refusing to make room for someone when asked to slide over.	• Confused • Stressed • Unhappy • Angry • Irritated • Sad	• Other people riding on the bus may notice and feel confused. • The driver and others may feel unsafe if someone is roaming around. • People might get angry if their chair is being kicked. • Everyone might be late for school if the driver has to stop for safety or to manage behaviors.	• Bad • Stressed • Confused • Uncomfortable • Angry • Frustrated
•	•	•	•
•	•	•	•

RIDING ON A PUBLIC BUS WITH STRANGERS
Behaviors That Are **EXPECTED** for the Situation

Behaviors, feelings, and possible actions or reactions are listed in categories in arbitrary order. There is not a one-to-one correlation between the information listed in each column. For example, whatever behavior is listed first does not have to match to the first feeling or action or reaction, and so on.

Expected Behaviors for the Situation	How Others Might Feel (or Think)	Possible Actions or Reactions	How the DOer Might Feel (or Think)
• Finding an open seat quickly or as soon as possible. • If there are no open seats, standing up and holding onto the handrail. • Staying seated once a seat is selected. • Pulling the stop cord or pressing the button in time for the driver to stop safely. • Sitting or standing near the driver for support in knowing when to exit the bus.	• Calm • Relaxed • Safe	• The DOer may reach their destination in a timely manner. • Other riders might leave the DOer alone to read or have quiet time. • The DOer may have a positive experience riding the bus. • The driver may feel like riders are being safe.	• Proud • Relaxed • Happy • Content • Pleased • Safe

Consider this:
How might this map change if you are the only person on the bus other than the driver?

RIDING ON A PUBLIC BUS WITH STRANGERS
Behaviors That Are **UNEXPECTED** for the Situation

Behaviors, feelings, and possible actions or reactions are listed in categories in arbitrary order. There is not a one-to-one correlation between the information listed in each column. For example, whatever behavior is listed first does not have to match to the first feeling or action or reaction, and so on.

Unexpected Behaviors for the Situation	How Others Might Feel (or Think)	Possible Actions or Reactions	How the DOer Might Feel (or Think)
• Taking a long time to pick a seat. • Yelling in a very loud voice. • Touching other people or their stuff. • Pulling the stop cord or pushing the button repeatedly.	• Confused • Stressed • Angry • Irritated • Frustrated • Unhappy	• Other people may notice and feel confused. • The bus may be late because the driver had to stop to take care of problems on the bus. • The driver may get frustrated and have to say something. • Other riders might feel unsafe.	• Stressed • Confused • Embarrassed • Frustrated • Unhappy • Unsafe
•	•	•	•
•	•	•	•

EATING IN THE SCHOOL CAFETERIA WITH PEERS
Behaviors That Are **EXPECTED** for the Situation

Behaviors, feelings, and possible actions or reactions are listed in categories in arbitrary order. There is not a one-to-one correlation between the information listed in each column. For example, whatever behavior is listed first does not have to match to the first feeling or action or reaction, and so on.

Expected Behaviors for the Situation	How Others Might Feel (or Think)	Possible Actions or Reactions	How the DOer Might Feel (or Think)
• Standing in line for food or bringing own lunch, then looking for open places to sit near familiar (or friendly) peers. • Siting an arm's length away from others (or ½ arm's length if it's crowded). • Chatting if desired, or just listening and/or showing attention to others with supportive comments (oh, cool, hmmm, really, wow). • Finding a quiet place to eat or asking a teacher if there is an empty classroom or study room if needed. • Throwing away trash in the trash can when finished. • •	• Calm • Comfortable • Relaxed • Happy → • •	• Everyone may be less likely to bump into each other. • People may enjoy eating and getting to know each other. • The area may be clean for the next people who need to use that area. • The DOer might feel proud that they advocated for their needs. → • •	• Proud • Happy • Comfortable • Calm • •

EATING IN THE SCHOOL CAFETERIA WITH PEERS
Behaviors That Are **UNEXPECTED** for the Situation

Behaviors, feelings, and possible actions or reactions are listed in categories in arbitrary order. There is not a one-to-one correlation between the information listed in each column. For example, whatever behavior is listed first does not have to match to the first feeling or action or reaction, and so on.

Unexpected Behaviors for the Situation	How Others Might Feel (or Think)	Possible Actions or Reactions	How the DOer Might Feel (or Think)
• Pushing to the front of the line. • Sitting where someone else already put their stuff or food down. • Shouting political, religious, racial, or other divisive opinions. • Wandering off campus or eating in off-limits areas without teacher permission. • Leaving trash all over the table or on the floor. • •	• Confused • Irritated • Angry • Frustrated • Grossed out → • •	• The DOer may be sent to the principal's office or back to class. • Others may avoid sitting with the DOer. • Others might be offended by the DOer's comments. → • •	• Embarrassed • Nervous • Lonely • Sad • Frustrated • •

Copyright © 2023 Think Social Publishing, Inc. All Rights Reserved. From the book, *Social Situation Mapping* by Winner and Crooke. www.socialthinking.com

COMPUTER OR TABLET ACTIVITIES AT SCHOOL
Behaviors That Are **EXPECTED** for the Situation

Behaviors, feelings, and possible actions or reactions are listed in categories in arbitrary order. There is not a one-to-one correlation between the information listed in each column. For example, whatever behavior is listed first does not have to match to the first feeling or action or reaction, and so on.

Expected Behaviors for the Situation	How Others Might Feel (or Think)	Possible Actions or Reactions	How the DOer Might Feel (or Think)
• Following the class rules about using tablets or computers. • If having problems with the equipment or are unclear about what to do, asking adults or other students to clarify. • Gently using the equipment. • Browsing or searching content that is relevant to the assignment. • Using assistive tools or technology, as needed.	• Calm • Happy • Focused • Ready to work	• The DOer may make good progress on the assignment. • The teacher might notice that the DOer is aware of the rules and following them. • The equipment may stay in good working order. • The teacher might allow for free time after the assignment is done.	• Focused • Happy • Proud • Calm

Consider this:
How might this map change if you were at home?

COMPUTER OR TABLET ACTIVITIES AT SCHOOL
Behaviors That Are **UNEXPECTED** for the Situation

Behaviors, feelings, and possible actions or reactions are listed in categories in arbitrary order. There is not a one-to-one correlation between the information listed in each column. For example, whatever behavior is listed first does not have to match to the first feeling or action or reaction, and so on.

Unexpected Behaviors for the Situation	How Others Might Feel (or Think)	Possible Actions or Reactions	How the DOer Might Feel (or Think)
• Playing computer games when there is an assignment to do. • Doing random internet searches during work time. • Ignoring the written/posted rules for working on technology. • Being rough on the computer or tablet. • Forgetting to advocate for sensory or other needs.	• Confused • Disappointed • Frustrated • Irritated • Angry • Stressed	• The DOer may not complete the assignment. • The teacher may restrict the DOer's computer/tablet time. • The technology might become unusable because of neglect. • The DOer may become overwhelmed or confused about what to do.	• Nervous • Embarrassed • Frustrated • Sad • Upset • Stressed

INITIATING PLAY WITH OTHERS AT SCHOOL
Behaviors That Are **EXPECTED** for the Situation

Behaviors, feelings, and possible actions or reactions are listed in categories in arbitrary order. There is not a one-to-one correlation between the information listed in each column. For example, whatever behavior is listed first does not have to match to the first feeling or action or reaction, and so on.

Expected Behaviors for the Situation	How Others Might Feel (or Think)	Possible Actions or Reactions	How the DOer Might Feel (or Think)
• Walking towards a group and standing an arm's length away. • Making supportive comments (or withholding negative comments) about the activity or the people. • Asking questions or making comments to show interest in joining the activity. • Being flexible and going along with rules that were already set. • Asking a trusted adult to help with strategies to initiate play with just one peer.	• Happy • Great • Understanding • Calm	• Others may notice the DOer would like to join. • Others may figure out the DOer's intentions and may invite them to play. • Everyone might have a good time playing together. • The DOer might gain practice in being around other kids and groups.	• Great • Happy • Proud • Calm • Ecstatic

Consider this:
How might this map change if you were at home or in a public space?

INITIATING PLAY WITH OTHERS AT SCHOOL
Behaviors That Are **UNEXPECTED** for the Situation

Behaviors, feelings, and possible actions or reactions are listed in categories in arbitrary order. There is not a one-to-one correlation between the information listed in each column. For example, whatever behavior is listed first does not have to match to the first feeling or action or reaction, and so on.

Unexpected Behaviors for the Situation	How Others Might Feel (or Think)	Possible Actions or Reactions	How the DOer Might Feel (or Think)
• Touching others or grabbing materials from others who are already playing. • Standing or staying far away from the group or activity the DOer wants to join. • Making new rules or refusing to play using the group rules. • Yelling at others if on the losing team. • •	• Confused • Angry • Frustrated • Angry → • •	• Others may think the DOer is trying to ruin their game. • Others may not realize the DOer wants to play. • The DOer may be ignored or asked to go away. • Others might avoid the DOer in the future. → • •	• Frustrated • Embarrassed • Lonely • Confused • Upset • •

SILENT READING IN THE CLASSROOM WITH PEERS
Behaviors That Are **EXPECTED** for the Situation

Behaviors, feelings, and possible actions or reactions are listed in categories in arbitrary order. There is not a one-to-one correlation between the information listed in each column. For example, whatever behavior is listed first does not have to match to the first feeling or action or reaction, and so on.

Expected Behaviors for the Situation	How Others Might Feel (or Think)	Possible Actions or Reactions	How the DOer Might Feel (or Think)
• Immediately taking out a book when the teacher says it's time for silent reading. • Reading for the entire silent reading time. • Reading silently or reading the words inside one's head rather than aloud. • Advocating for using assistive tools to help with focus or asking to read in a sensory-friendly area.	• Calm • Happy • Relaxed • Proud of you	• The DOer may have more time to read. • Everyone may enjoy quiet reading time. • The teacher may notice that the DOer is prepared and understands the unspoken rules of silent reading time. • The teacher may make a positive comment about how the DOer is advocating for how they learn best.	• Proud • Happy • Relaxed • Calm

Consider this:
How might this map change if you were in the public library with others?

SILENT READING IN THE CLASSROOM WITH PEERS
Behaviors That Are **UNEXPECTED** for the Situation

Behaviors, feelings, and possible actions or reactions are listed in categories in arbitrary order. There is not a one-to-one correlation between the information listed in each column. For example, whatever behavior is listed first does not have to match to the first feeling or action or reaction, and so on.

Unexpected Behaviors for the Situation	How Others Might Feel (or Think)	Possible Actions or Reactions	How the DOer Might Feel (or Think)
• Reading the book aloud when sharing space with others. • Doing something else when the teacher says it's time for silent reading. • Continuing to read when silent reading is over. • Leaving the room without permission.	• Confused • Frustrated • Disappointed • Angry • Nervous • Frustrated	• Other students might notice and avoid other activities with the DOer. • The DOer may miss out on reading time. • The teacher may be frustrated and ask the DOer to leave. • The teacher might call the parent or caregiver.	• Frustrated • Disturbed • Embarrassed • Uncomfortable • Sad • Stressed
•	•	•	•
•	•	•	•

PARTICIPATING IN ART CLASS WITH CLASSMATES
Behaviors That Are **EXPECTED** for the Situation

Behaviors, feelings, and possible actions or reactions are listed in categories in arbitrary order. There is not a one-to-one correlation between the information listed in each column. For example, whatever behavior is listed first does not have to match to the first feeling or action or reaction, and so on.

Expected Behaviors for the Situation	How Others Might Feel (or Think)	Possible Actions or Reactions	How the DOer Might Feel (or Think)
• Following classroom rules for using art materials. • Asking the teacher or others if confused about what to do. • Gathering only the materials needed for their project. • Using the materials as they were intended (paint brush for paint, glue for securing items, etc.). • Asking to use materials that are sensory-friendly (different texture, smell, etc.).	• Calm • Happy • Focused • Able to work	• The DOer might have more time to complete their project. • The teacher might notice that the DOer is aware of and following the rules for art class. • Others have enough materials to do their own projects. • Teachers and parents might be proud that students are advocating for tools to complete the task in a manner that works for them.	• Proud • Happy • Creative • Calm

Consider this:
How might this map change if you were taking an online art class with others?

PARTICIPATING IN ART CLASS WITH CLASSMATES
Behaviors That Are **UNEXPECTED** for the Situation

Behaviors, feelings, and possible actions or reactions are listed in categories in arbitrary order. There is not a one-to-one correlation between the information listed in each column. For example, whatever behavior is listed first does not have to match to the first feeling or action or reaction, and so on.

Unexpected Behaviors for the Situation	How Others Might Feel (or Think)	Possible Actions or Reactions	How the DOer Might Feel (or Think)
• Creating an art project that is unrelated to the assignment. • Critiquing another's art when not asked. • Touching others' materials or art pieces. • Refusing to participate in any way.	• Confused • Annoyed • Frustrated • Impatient • Uncomfortable • Stressed	• The DOer might get a poor grade. • The teacher may ask the DOer to focus on their own work. • The DOer may not have time to finish their project. • Other's might be embarrassed or offended.	• Frustrated • Embarrassed • Uncomfortable • Nervous • Pressured

FREE TIME IN CLASS
Behaviors That Are EXPECTED for the Situation
(For times when you finish classwork early or the teacher gives you free time)

Behaviors, feelings, and possible actions or reactions are listed in categories in arbitrary order. There is not a one-to-one correlation between the information listed in each column. For example, whatever behavior is listed first does not have to match to the first feeling or action or reaction, and so on.

Expected Behaviors for the Situation	How Others Might Feel (or Think)	Possible Actions or Reactions	How the DOer Might Feel (or Think)
• Asking teacher what can be done if all assigned work is finished. • Finishing work for another class. • Reading silently or drawing if that's allowed. • Meditating, taking some deep breaths, or quietly stretching in seat or using a fidget to prepare for the next lesson. • Asking teacher for a movement break. • •	• Calm • Relaxed • Happy • Proud of you → • •	• Teacher may offer a positive comment. • The DOer may get other homework finished early. • Others may notice that the DOer is managing their time. • The DOer might feel proud they are using their strategies. → • •	• Proud • Happy • Great • Ready for the next activity • Productive • •

FREE TIME IN CLASS
Behaviors That Are **UNEXPECTED** for the Situation
(For times when you finish classwork early or the teacher gives you free time)

Behaviors, feelings, and possible actions or reactions are listed in categories in arbitrary order. There is not a one-to-one correlation between the information listed in each column. For example, whatever behavior is listed first does not have to match to the first feeling or action or reaction, and so on.

Unexpected Behaviors for the Situation	How Others Might Feel (or Think)	Possible Actions or Reactions	How the DOer Might Feel (or Think)
• Talking or bothering others when they are still working. • Rustling papers, banging pencils, or making loud noises rather than using fidgets or other strategies. • Wandering around the classroom without permission. • Touching others or touching their property.	• Confused • Irritated • Frustrated • Distracted • Nervous • Angry	• The teacher may notice and make a corrective or negative comment. • The teacher may contact the parent or guardian. • Others may be distracted and unable to finish their work. • Others may become angry or frustrated.	• Embarrassed • Frustrated • Uncomfortable • Sad • Stressed
• •	→ • •	→ • •	• •

UNSCHEDULED OR WAITING TIME AT SCHOOL
Behaviors That Are **EXPECTED** for the Situation

Behaviors, feelings, and possible actions or reactions are listed in categories in arbitrary order. There is not a one-to-one correlation between the information listed in each column. For example, whatever behavior is listed first does not have to match to the first feeling or action or reaction, and so on.

Expected Behaviors for the Situation	How Others Might Feel (or Think)	Possible Actions or Reactions	How the DOer Might Feel (or Think)
• Working or talking quietly to others nearby. • Reading a book. • Noticing when the teacher changes the plan (announcement or writing plan on the board). • Drawing or catching up on other work. • Using fidgets or other tools and strategies to stay relaxed and connected to the group plan.	• Calm • Relaxed • Friendly	• The teacher might notice that the DOer is aware of choices for waiting time. • The teacher might make a positive comment. • Others can make their own choices without distraction. • The DOer might get practice at surviving the boring moment or dealing with down time.	• Responsible • Relaxed • Prepared • Ready to work • Productive

Consider this:
How might this map change if you were home? What about if an adult was not around while you were waiting?

UNSCHEDULED OR WAITING TIME AT SCHOOL
Behaviors That Are **UNEXPECTED** for the Situation

Behaviors, feelings, and possible actions or reactions are listed in categories in arbitrary order. There is not a one-to-one correlation between the information listed in each column. For example, whatever behavior is listed first does not have to match to the first feeling or action or reaction, and so on.

Unexpected Behaviors for the Situation	How Others Might Feel (or Think)	Possible Actions or Reactions	How the DOer Might Feel (or Think)
• Repeatedly asking the teacher or others what to do. • Wandering around the room without permission. • Yelling across the room. • Distracting others who are managing their own downtime. • Get "stuck" on one's own plan even after the teacher states a new group plan. • •	• Confused • Annoyed • Irritated • Distracted → • •	• The teacher notices the DOer is following their own plan. • Others might get distracted and feel upset. • Teacher may be frustrated and correct the DOer. → • •	• Anxious • Frustrated • Distracted • Unhappy • •

GETTING READY AND PLAYING AT RECESS WITH OTHERS
Behaviors That Are **EXPECTED** for the Situation

Behaviors, feelings, and possible actions or reactions are listed in categories in arbitrary order. There is not a one-to-one correlation between the information listed in each column. For example, whatever behavior is listed first does not have to match to the first feeling or action or reaction, and so on.

Expected Behaviors for the Situation	How Others Might Feel (or Think)	Possible Actions or Reactions	How the DOer Might Feel (or Think)
• Lining up to go to the playground or courtyard. • Inviting one or more kids to play a game. • Using eyes, brain, and body to observe what others are doing and using words to ask to join in. • Asking a trusted adult to help with strategies for joining a game or helping to organize an inside game with fewer peers.	• Friendly • Happy • Engaged • Like they are having fun	• Others might notice the DOer wants to join the play or the game. • Others might feel included if the DOer invites them to play. • The DOer might get practice in advocating play with one or more peers.	• Proud • Happy • Calm • Friendly

Consider this:
How might this map change if there was no teacher around but you were still supposed to line up?

GETTING READY AND PLAYING AT RECESS WITH OTHERS
Behaviors That Are **UNEXPECTED** for the Situation

Behaviors, feelings, and possible actions or reactions are listed in categories in arbitrary order. There is not a one-to-one correlation between the information listed in each column. For example, whatever behavior is listed first does not have to match to the first feeling or action or reaction, and so on.

Unexpected Behaviors for the Situation	How Others Might Feel (or Think)	Possible Actions or Reactions	How the DOer Might Feel (or Think)
• Joining a game and immediately making new rules. • Taking equipment or touching materials others are using. • Yelling and/or accusing others when losing a game. • Hiding or refusing to take a body and brain break.	• Confused because it's expected that you will learn the rules • Frustrated • Impatient • Annoyed • Stressed	• The DOer may be asked to leave the playground or not invited to join the game. • People might be frustrated that the DOer touched or took their equipment. • Others may avoid playing or hanging out with the DOer in the future. • The teacher may contact the parent or caregiver.	• Frustrated • Embarrassed • Uncomfortable • Lonely • Sad
•	•	•	•
•	•	•	•

Copyright © 2023 Think Social Publishing, Inc. All Rights Reserved. From the book, *Social Situation Mapping* by Winner and Crooke. www.socialthinking.com

STANDING IN LINE WITH OTHERS AT SCHOOL
Behaviors That Are **EXPECTED** for the Situation

Behaviors, feelings, and possible actions or reactions are listed in categories in arbitrary order. There is not a one-to-one correlation between the information listed in each column. For example, whatever behavior is listed first does not have to match to the first feeling or action or reaction, and so on.

Expected Behaviors for the Situation	How Others Might Feel (or Think)	Possible Actions or Reactions	How the DOer Might Feel (or Think)
• Standing about one arm's length away from others. • Being alert to hear the teacher's instructions or watching others to figure out what to do. • Keeping one's body in the group when the line moves. • Using a fidget or other tool to avoid touching others. • Practicing being in the front, middle, or end of the line.	• Calm • Comfortable • Happy • Safe	• Everyone is less likely to bump into each other. • The teacher may notice the DOer is using their tools. • The DOer will hear when the teacher makes announcements.	• Proud • Comfortable • Confident • Calm

Consider this:
How might this map change if you were in line at a store? What about lining up to be picked for a team?

STANDING IN LINE WITH OTHERS AT SCHOOL
Behaviors That Are **UNEXPECTED** for the Situation

Behaviors, feelings, and possible actions or reactions are listed in categories in arbitrary order. There is not a one-to-one correlation between the information listed in each column. For example, whatever behavior is listed first does not have to match to the first feeling or action or reaction, and so on.

Unexpected Behaviors for the Situation	How Others Might Feel (or Think)	Possible Actions or Reactions	How the DOer Might Feel (or Think)
• Bumping into or getting into others' personal space (touching or standing too close). • Talking at the same time the teacher is giving instructions. • Doing one's own plan rather than following the group plan. • Insisting on being first in line and getting upset if someone else is first. • •	• Confused • Nervous • Angry • Irritated • Stressed → • •	• Others may notice if the DOer is bumping into them and have to move away. • The teacher may notice and speak to the DOer about what they are doing or saying. • Others might get distracted and miss important information. • Delays in getting to the next activity might happen. → • •	• Embarrassed • Uncomfortable • Nervous • Frustrated • Pressured • •

WAITING FOR THE TEACHER TO START CLASS
Behaviors That Are **EXPECTED** for the Situation

Behaviors, feelings, and possible actions or reactions are listed in categories in arbitrary order. There is not a one-to-one correlation between the information listed in each column. For example, whatever behavior is listed first does not have to match to the first feeling or action or reaction, and so on.

Expected Behaviors for the Situation	How Others Might Feel (or Think)	Possible Actions or Reactions	How the DOer Might Feel (or Think)
• Looking at the board for the written schedule. • Taking out needed materials for the next activity. • If not sure what to do, looking at what others are doing. • Talking quietly, reading silently, or using sensory tools or strategies while waiting. • •	• Calm • Relaxed • Attentive → •	• The teacher might notice how students are using their tools or strategies. • Everyone will be ready once the lesson starts. → •	• Responsible • Relaxed • Prepared • Ready to work •

WAITING FOR THE TEACHER TO START CLASS
Behaviors That Are **UNEXPECTED** for the Situation

Behaviors, feelings, and possible actions or reactions are listed in categories in arbitrary order. There is not a one-to-one correlation between the information listed in each column. For example, whatever behavior is listed first does not have to match to the first feeling or action or reaction, and so on.

Unexpected Behaviors for the Situation	How Others Might Feel (or Think)	Possible Actions or Reactions	How the DOer Might Feel (or Think)
• Yelling or stating about how boring it is to wait. • Wandering around the room without permission. • Leaving the classroom.	• Confused • Annoyed • Irritated • Distracted	• The teacher may make statements to correct the DOer's behaviors. • Others may be distracted or be frustrated. • The principal, parent, or caregiver might get a phone call about the DOer's behaviors.	• Anxious • Frustrated • Left out • Distracted

INDEPENDENT DESK WORK IN CLASS
Behaviors That Are **EXPECTED** for the Situation

Behaviors, feelings, and possible actions or reactions are listed in categories in arbitrary order. There is not a one-to-one correlation between the information listed in each column. For example, whatever behavior is listed first does not have to match to the first feeling or action or reaction, and so on.

Expected Behaviors for the Situation	How Others Might Feel (or Think)	Possible Actions or Reactions	How the DOer Might Feel (or Think)
• Working quietly without distracting others (using fidgets or other tools/strategies). • If stuck or distracted by others, asking the teacher to allow work to occur in another area with fewer distractions. • When finished with one project, either work on an assignment from another class or silently read a book.	• Relaxed • Productive • Helpful • Calm	• Others can also work independently without getting distracted. • Teacher may notice the DOer is using their strategies and tools. • The DOer may get a chance to finish homework from another class or read.	• Calm • Proud • Relaxed • Successful

Consider this:
How might this map change if you were doing independent work at home?

INDEPENDENT DESK WORK IN CLASS
Behaviors That Are **UNEXPECTED** for the Situation

Behaviors, feelings, and possible actions or reactions are listed in categories in arbitrary order. There is not a one-to-one correlation between the information listed in each column. For example, whatever behavior is listed first does not have to match to the first feeling or action or reaction, and so on.

Unexpected Behaviors for the Situation	How Others Might Feel (or Think)	Possible Actions or Reactions	How the DOer Might Feel (or Think)
• Touching others' materials. • Wandering around the classroom without permission. • Stating aloud, "This is boring." • Refusing to do the assignment. • •	• Confused • Bothered • Irritated • Annoyed • Angry → • •	• Others may tell the DOer to stop or be quiet. • Others may avoid the DOer in the future because they feel angry or frustrated. • Teacher may think the DOer doesn't care about learning. • The DOer may not learn the material or finish their assignment. • The teacher may ask the DOer to focus on their work. → • •	• Embarrassed • Frustrated • Lonely • Sad • •

Copyright © 2023 Think Social Publishing, Inc. All Rights Reserved. From the book, *Social Situation Mapping* by Winner and Crooke. www.socialthinking.com

PARTICIPATING IN CLASS DISCUSSIONS
Behaviors That Are **EXPECTED** for the Situation

Behaviors, feelings, and possible actions or reactions are listed in categories in arbitrary order. There is not a one-to-one correlation between the information listed in each column. For example, whatever behavior is listed first does not have to match to the first feeling or action or reaction, and so on.

Expected Behaviors for the Situation	How Others Might Feel (or Think)	Possible Actions or Reactions	How the DOer Might Feel (or Think)
• Making comments and asking questions related to the topic of discussion. • Using brain and eyes to think about what the teacher and other students are saying or showing. • If not satisfied with a teacher's style of teaching, use a "brain filter" to keep comments in one's head. • Use a thought journal to log critical or corrective thoughts about peers or the teacher.	• Interested • Calm • Relaxed • Involved	• The teachers may notice the DOer is contributing to the group discussion. • Other students may notice the DOer is a part of the learning group. • Other students might learn how much knowledge the DOer has about the topic.	• Part of the group • Proud • Relaxed • Successful

Consider this:
How might this map change if this was an online class?

PARTICIPATING IN CLASS DISCUSSIONS
Behaviors That Are **UNEXPECTED** for the Situation

Behaviors, feelings, and possible actions or reactions are listed in categories in arbitrary order. There is not a one-to-one correlation between the information listed in each column. For example, whatever behavior is listed first does not have to match to the first feeling or action or reaction, and so on.

Unexpected Behaviors for the Situation	How Others Might Feel (or Think)	Possible Actions or Reactions	How the DOer Might Feel (or Think)
• Adding thoughts or comments unrelated to the discussion or only about personal interests. • Turning away from the group or leaving the classroom. • Telling others their comments are stupid or wrong. • Telling the teacher they are boring or the topic is not interesting. • •	• Confused • Irritated • Annoyed • Hostile → • •	• Others may be confused or offended. • The teacher may wonder if the DOer is thinking about the topic being discussed. • Others may feel ignored or disregarded. • Others may not enjoy the DOer being part of the group. → • •	• Embarrassed • Frustrated • Left out • Anxious • Sad • •

NOTE-TAKING DURING CLASS TIME
Behaviors That Are **EXPECTED** for the Situation

Behaviors, feelings, and possible actions or reactions are listed in categories in arbitrary order. There is not a one-to-one correlation between the information listed in each column. For example, whatever behavior is listed first does not have to match to the first feeling or action or reaction, and so on.

Expected Behaviors for the Situation	How Others Might Feel (or Think)	Possible Actions or Reactions	How the DOer Might Feel (or Think)
• Using an outline, short sentences, visual diagrams, mind maps, etc. • Asking for clarification after the teacher is done presenting if confused about a concept. • Writing down the main points and adding relevant details. • Advocating for help in note-taking (Asking for a notetaker or copies of an outline or notes).	• Confident • Proud • Calm	• Others may be willing to share their notes with the DOer. • The teacher may notice the DOer using their tools and strategies. • The DOer might gain practice in note-taking and/or be prepared to study or take a test.	• Calm • Confident • Relaxed • Proud

Consider this:
How might this map change if you were taking notes at home from a book?

NOTE-TAKING DURING CLASS TIME
Behaviors That Are **UNEXPECTED** for the Situation

Behaviors, feelings, and possible actions or reactions are listed in categories in arbitrary order. There is not a one-to-one correlation between the information listed in each column. For example, whatever behavior is listed first does not have to match to the first feeling or action or reaction, and so on.

Unexpected Behaviors for the Situation	How Others Might Feel (or Think)	Possible Actions or Reactions	How the DOer Might Feel (or Think)
• Doodling and/or drawing instead of taking notes. • Refusing to ask for help or avoiding advocating for oneself (even after given strategies to do so). • Trying to write down every word.	• Confused • They think I'm lazy. • They think I'm not interested. • Frustrated	• The DOer may have trouble studying without good notes. • The DOer may become overwhelmed. • Other students may think the DOer doesn't care about school. • The teacher may notice the DOer is making choices that do not help them to learn.	• Frustrated • Lonely • Confused • A failure
•	•	•	•
•	•	•	•

USING THE BATHROOM AT SCHOOL
Behaviors That Are **EXPECTED** for the Situation

Behaviors, feelings, and possible actions or reactions are listed in categories in arbitrary order. There is not a one-to-one correlation between the information listed in each column. For example, whatever behavior is listed first does not have to match to the first feeling or action or reaction, and so on.

Expected Behaviors for the Situation	How Others Might Feel (or Think)	Possible Actions or Reactions	How the DOer Might Feel (or Think)
• Remembering to try to use the bathroom during class breaks or between classes. • If leaving class, directly going to the bathroom and returning to class quickly. • If needing a break, using strategies for taking a break rather than using the bathroom as the break area. • Quietly leaving and returning to the classroom and quickly joining the class activity.	• Able to work • Calm • Productive	• Others can continue working without being interrupted. • The teacher might notice that students are only leaving the class for the bathroom when needed. • The DOer knows they can use their break strategy without having to use the bathroom as their break area.	• Responsible • Relaxed • Successful

Consider this: How might this map change if you were attending an online class?

USING THE BATHROOM AT SCHOOL
Behaviors That Are **UNEXPECTED** for the Situation

Behaviors, feelings, and possible actions or reactions are listed in categories in arbitrary order. There is not a one-to-one correlation between the information listed in each column. For example, whatever behavior is listed first does not have to match to the first feeling or action or reaction, and so on.

Unexpected Behaviors for the Situation	How Others Might Feel (or Think)	Possible Actions or Reactions	How the DOer Might Feel (or Think)
• Repeatedly leaving the class to use the bathroom. • Requesting to go to the bathroom because of boredom or avoiding schoolwork. • Taking a really long time to return to the classroom. • Announcing in a loud voice when leaving or re-entering the classroom. • Leaving the classroom without asking or telling the teacher. • •	• Confused • Annoyed • Irritated • Distracted → • •	• The teacher may think the DOer is trying to skip class. • Others might notice and wonder why the DOer leaves class so often. • Others may be distracted if the DOer is loud when they are leaving or returning. • Caregivers or parents might be contacted. → • •	• Anxious • Inattentive • Left out • •

GETTING INTO A WORK GROUP WITH PEERS IN CLASS
Behaviors That Are **EXPECTED** for the Situation

Behaviors, feelings, and possible actions or reactions are listed in categories in arbitrary order. There is not a one-to-one correlation between the information listed in each column. For example, whatever behavior is listed first does not have to match to the first feeling or action or reaction, and so on.

Expected Behaviors for the Situation	How Others Might Feel (or Think)	Possible Actions or Reactions	How the DOer Might Feel (or Think)
• Noticing which groups still need a person. • Moving towards a group and using words to show one's desire to join the group ("looks like you need another for your group, I'll join your group, etc.). • Moving to another group if the current one is full. • Noticing and inviting others to join the group. • If finding, joining, or working in groups is difficult, advocating and explaining to the teacher in advance. • •	• Fine • Calm • Pleased → • •	• The DOer may feel included in the classroom activities. • The DOer might get practice in joining and working in groups. • The DOer may learn to join and invite others to work together. • The teacher might praise the student for using their advocacy skills. → • •	• Productive • Relaxed • Prepared • Calm • Connected • •

GETTING INTO A WORK GROUP WITH PEERS IN CLASS
Behaviors That Are **UNEXPECTED** for the Situation

Behaviors, feelings, and possible actions or reactions are listed in categories in arbitrary order. There is not a one-to-one correlation between the information listed in each column. For example, whatever behavior is listed first does not have to match to the first feeling or action or reaction, and so on.

Unexpected Behaviors for the Situation	How Others Might Feel (or Think)	Possible Actions or Reactions	How the DOer Might Feel (or Think)
• Refusing to work in a group or advocate for one's own needs related to groups. • Ignoring others who might want to join a group. • Telling others in the group they are not smart, clever, or useful in the group. • • •	• Confused • Annoyed • Rejected • Stressed • Disgusted → • •	• Others may notice the DOer refusing to be a part of a group and avoid asking them in the future. • Others might be offended by the DOer's comments about the group. • The teacher may not know about the DOer's needs around working in groups and assume they don't care about learning. → • •	• Frustrated • Angry • Depressed • Rejected • Uncomfortable • Anxious • •

Copyright © 2023 Think Social Publishing, Inc. All Rights Reserved. From the book, *Social Situation Mapping* by Winner and Crooke. www.socialthinking.com

WORKING IN A SMALL GROUP WITH PEERS IN CLASS
Behaviors That Are **EXPECTED** for the Situation

Behaviors, feelings, and possible actions or reactions are listed in categories in arbitrary order. There is not a one-to-one correlation between the information listed in each column. For example, whatever behavior is listed first does not have to match to the first feeling or action or reaction, and so on.

Expected Behaviors for the Situation	How Others Might Feel (or Think)	Possible Actions or Reactions	How the DOer Might Feel (or Think)
• Contributing to the group with questions and comments. • Noticing the amount of time people get to make comments and using about the same amount of time. • Keeping critiques and negative comments about others' opinions or thoughts to a minimum (or none). • Being flexible about changes to the group plan. • Advocating for working in a pair/dyad if the sensory load of a group is too much. • •	• Calm • Productive • Included • Confident • Connected → • •	• The teacher might notice and comment on how well the group is working. • The group may make progress on the work. • Everyone may feel more comfortable sharing their ideas. • The final product may reflect all persons' ideas working together. → • •	• Productive • Relaxed • Prepared • Calm • Connected • •

WORKING IN A SMALL GROUP WITH PEERS IN CLASS
Behaviors That Are **UNEXPECTED** for the Situation

Behaviors, feelings, and possible actions or reactions are listed in categories in arbitrary order. There is not a one-to-one correlation between the information listed in each column. For example, whatever behavior is listed first does not have to match to the first feeling or action or reaction, and so on.

Unexpected Behaviors for the Situation	How Others Might Feel (or Think)	Possible Actions or Reactions	How the DOer Might Feel (or Think)
• Having an idea but staying silent. • Dominating the conversation and not letting others talk. • Criticizing others' ideas. • Being inflexible about how the group will complete the project. • •	• Confused • Annoyed • Frustrated • Bored • Angry • Hurt → • •	• Others may think the DOer isn't a good group partner. • Others may not want to work with the DOer next time. • Others in the group may get frustrated or become impatient with the DOer. • The group may not finish. → • •	• Anxious • Frustrated • Left out • Sad • Unsuccessful • •

PREPARING TO LEAVE A CLASS EACH DAY
Behaviors That Are **EXPECTED** for the Situation

Behaviors, feelings, and possible actions or reactions are listed in categories in arbitrary order. There is not a one-to-one correlation between the information listed in each column. For example, whatever behavior is listed first does not have to match to the first feeling or action or reaction, and so on.

Expected Behaviors for the Situation	How Others Might Feel (or Think)	Possible Actions or Reactions	How the DOer Might Feel (or Think)
• Thinking "What is the homework for tonight?" from the time class begins. • Writing down an assignment as soon as it is announced or checking the homework requirements online each night. • If confused during class, asking questions or writing down questions to ask later. • Gathering all personal materials and putting them into a backpack or bag. • Advocating for help developing a system of reminders. • •	• Confident • Pleased • Relaxed → • •	• Teachers may notice the DOer's efforts and make a positive comment. • Parents or caregivers may notice the DOer knows what homework is needed for each class. • The teacher may think the DOer is interested in learning and being part of the group. • The DOer will have their backpack and other personal items ready for the next class or to take home. → • •	• Pleased • Confident • Proud • •

PREPARING TO LEAVE A CLASS EACH DAY
Behaviors That Are **UNEXPECTED** for the Situation

Behaviors, feelings, and possible actions or reactions are listed in categories in arbitrary order. There is not a one-to-one correlation between the information listed in each column. For example, whatever behavior is listed first does not have to match to the first feeling or action or reaction, and so on.

Unexpected Behaviors for the Situation	How Others Might Feel (or Think)	Possible Actions or Reactions	How the DOer Might Feel (or Think)
• Ignoring when a teacher gives an assignment. • Refusing to check online for assignments. • Feeling confused about the assignment and leaving that class without asking for clarification. • Refusing help to develop or learn strategies for organizing materials.	• Confused • Irritated • Annoyed • Discouraged • Apathetic	• Teacher may be frustrated that the DOer doesn't know or ask about homework assignments. • Others may think the DOer is not interested in learning. • Parents or caregivers may be upset that the DOer isn't tracking homework assignments. • The DOer may not finish their work and end up with poor grades.	• Overwhelmed • Defeated • Incapable • Sad
•	•	•	•
•	•	•	•

TIME BETWEEN CLASSES WITH PEERS (ADULTS NOT AROUND)
Behaviors That Are **EXPECTED** for the Situation

Behaviors, feelings, and possible actions or reactions are listed in categories in arbitrary order. There is not a one-to-one correlation between the information listed in each column. For example, whatever behavior is listed first does not have to match to the first feeling or action or reaction, and so on.

Expected Behaviors for the Situation	How Others Might Feel (or Think)	Possible Actions or Reactions	How the DOer Might Feel (or Think)
• Noticing who is around and what is going on. • Being silly or joking around with friends or friendly peers while waiting. • If technology is allowed, checking email, social media, or watching online videos. • Avoiding peers who have been unfriendly or are bullies. • Taking care of personal needs (have a snack, take a sensory break, go to the bathroom).	• Relaxed • Friendly • Happy • Calm	• The DOer won't bump into others and may notice if someone wants to chat. • Others may notice or think the DOer is friendly. • Students may give other students space to take care of their personal needs. • Others may start a conversation or include the DOer in their group.	• Ready • Pleased • Accepted • Included

Consider this:
How might this map look different if the break was for online classes?

TIME BETWEEN CLASSES WITH PEERS
(ADULTS NOT AROUND)
Behaviors That Are **UNEXPECTED** for the Situation

Behaviors, feelings, and possible actions or reactions are listed in categories in arbitrary order. There is not a one-to-one correlation between the information listed in each column. For example, whatever behavior is listed first does not have to match to the first feeling or action or reaction, and so on.

Unexpected Behaviors for the Situation	How Others Might Feel (or Think)	Possible Actions or Reactions	How the DOer Might Feel (or Think)
• Walking quickly between classes without noticing who is in the path. • Ignoring friends and familiar people. • Grabbing or touching others' technology or personal items without asking. • Ignoring body signals indicating hunger, anxiety, or overload. • Seeking out or trying to interact with bullies or people who have been mean in the past. • •	• Confused • Angry • Ignored • Irritated • Annoyed → • •	• Others may think the DOer is unfriendly or doesn't like them. • The DOer may bump into others and cause frustration. • Others may be confused or upset if others touch their stuff. → • •	• Sad • Stressed • Lonely • Rejected • •

PREPARING TO GO HOME FROM SCHOOL
Behaviors That Are **EXPECTED** for the Situation

Behaviors, feelings, and possible actions or reactions are listed in categories in arbitrary order. There is not a one-to-one correlation between the information listed in each column. For example, whatever behavior is listed first does not have to match to the first feeling or action or reaction, and so on.

Expected Behaviors for the Situation	How Others Might Feel (or Think)	Possible Actions or Reactions	How the DOer Might Feel (or Think)
• Organizing books together in the same place (backpack, locker, desk, assigned shelf). • Using a planner or other tools to figure out what materials to bring home for homework. • Looking at board or checking online to confirm assignments or important notes. • Following the end of day routine (e.g., putting chair on top of desk, throwing away trash nearby, putting items away, etc.). • •	• Pleased • Calm • Happy • Relieved → • •	• The teacher may notice the DOer is getting prepared and make a positive comment. • The DOer may be able to complete all their assignments because they have what they need. • The DOer's parents or caregivers may be pleased the DOer is prepared. • The cleaning staff may notice the effort and feel grateful. → • •	• Calm • Confident • Responsible • •

46 Copyright © 2023 Think Social Publishing, Inc. All Rights Reserved. From the book, *Social Situation Mapping* by Winner and Crooke. www.socialthinking.com

PREPARING TO GO HOME FROM SCHOOL
Behaviors That Are **UNEXPECTED** for the Situation

Behaviors, feelings, and possible actions or reactions are listed in categories in arbitrary order. There is not a one-to-one correlation between the information listed in each column. For example, whatever behavior is listed first does not have to match to the first feeling or action or reaction, and so on.

Unexpected Behaviors for the Situation	How Others Might Feel (or Think)	Possible Actions or Reactions	How the DOer Might Feel (or Think)
• Tossing or leaving papers, books, or materials around the room or creating messes before leaving. • Refusing to use a planner or other tool to figure out what needs to go home. • Relying only on memory to know what is due. • Refusing to follow the end of day routine. • •	• Confused • Annoyed • Frustrated • Disappointed → • •	• The teacher may contact the DOer's parents or caregivers. • The teacher may be confused as to why the DOer isn't using their planner. • The DOer may not have their homework ready for class the next day. • The teacher may give the whole class consequences for leaving the room a mess. → • •	• Embarrassed • Angry • Surprised • Anxious • Nervous • •

THINKING ABOUT SCHOOLWORK AT HOME
Behaviors That Are **EXPECTED** for the Situation

Behaviors, feelings, and possible actions or reactions are listed in categories in arbitrary order. There is not a one-to-one correlation between the information listed in each column. For example, whatever behavior is listed first does not have to match to the first feeling or action or reaction, and so on.

Expected Behaviors for the Situation	How Others Might Feel (or Think)	Possible Actions or Reactions	How the DOer Might Feel (or Think)
• Being aware that everyone has to do schoolwork they like as well as the work they don't like. • Using an inner coach to help get started or stay positive about getting work done. • If worried or anxious about schoolwork, talking to a trusted adult. • Making a plan to start and finish the hardest things first to get them out of the way. • Using positive self-talk ("you can do this!"). • •	• Proud • Calm • Happy → • •	• The DOer may feel like they have a plan to get things done. • The DOer might be more relaxed knowing they have someone to talk to when worried. • The DOer might enjoy thinking about what to do for fun when schoolwork is finished. • The DOer might get practice using their inner positive voice. → • •	• Happy • Proud • Relaxed • Successful • •

THINKING ABOUT SCHOOLWORK AT HOME
Behaviors That Are **UNEXPECTED** for the Situation

Behaviors, feelings, and possible actions or reactions are listed in categories in arbitrary order. There is not a one-to-one correlation between the information listed in each column. For example, whatever behavior is listed first does not have to match to the first feeling or action or reaction, and so on.

Unexpected Behaviors for the Situation	How Others Might Feel (or Think)	Possible Actions or Reactions	How the DOer Might Feel (or Think)
• Paying attention to negative thoughts about schoolwork. ("I hate this subject…") • Listening to the inner critic about oneself. ("You are never any good at this…") • Keeping worries or concerns about schoolwork inside. • Lying to parents about not having schoolwork to complete.	• Confused • Angry • Frustrated • Worried	• The DOer may become more negative about schoolwork and themselves. • The DOer may get behind or feel overwhelmed. • The DOer may get negative consequences for lying.	• Annoyed • Angry • Sad

ACTUAL TIME DOING HOMEWORK
Behaviors That Are EXPECTED for the Situation

Behaviors, feelings, and possible actions or reactions are listed in categories in arbitrary order. There is not a one-to-one correlation between the information listed in each column. For example, whatever behavior is listed first does not have to match to the first feeling or action or reaction, and so on.

Expected Behaviors for the Situation	How Others Might Feel (or Think)	Possible Actions or Reactions	How the DOer Might Feel (or Think)
• Making a daily plan by ordering assignment priority and estimating the time each task will take, including some breaks. • Starting the work early enough to have fun time before bed. • Using tools to keep track of time such as digital or manual alarms or timers. • Finding a good place to do homework where distractions are minimal. • •	• Relaxed • Proud • Calm → •	• The DOer may be getting work completed efficiently. • Parents or caregivers may notice the DOer is managing their time and offer positive comments. • The DOer may have free time before bed and plenty of time to sleep. • The DOer might gain skills in time prediction. → •	• Happy • Proud • Relaxed •

ACTUAL TIME DOING HOMEWORK
Behaviors That Are **UNEXPECTED** for the Situation

Behaviors, feelings, and possible actions or reactions are listed in categories in arbitrary order. There is not a one-to-one correlation between the information listed in each column. For example, whatever behavior is listed first does not have to match to the first feeling or action or reaction, and so on.

Unexpected Behaviors for the Situation	How Others Might Feel (or Think)	Possible Actions or Reactions	How the DOer Might Feel (or Think)
• Putting off homework until right before bed. • Picking assignments at random without a plan. • Ignoring clock, alarms, or timers. • Trying to do homework in distracting places (near video game, TV, etc.)	• Confused • Frustrated • Exhausted • Angry	• Parents may have to constantly remind the DOer to focus on their work. • The DOer may feel exhausted by staying up too late to work. • The DOer may not work efficiently because there are so many distractions.	• Angry • Tired • Frustrated • Unsuccessful
•	•	•	•
•	•	•	•

STUDYING AT HOME
(PARENTS OR CAREGIVERS ARE PRESENT)
Behaviors That Are **EXPECTED** for the Situation

Behaviors, feelings, and possible actions or reactions are listed in categories in arbitrary order. There is not a one-to-one correlation between the information listed in each column. For example, whatever behavior is listed first does not have to match to the first feeling or action or reaction, and so on.

Expected Behaviors for the Situation	How Others Might Feel (or Think)	Possible Actions or Reactions	How the DOer Might Feel (or Think)
• Knowing that studying for tests must be part of homework time. • Once a test is announced, setting up a consistent study schedule. • Advocating for oneself to get help in note-taking or study skills. • Using study tools (mind maps, highlighters, lists, index cards).	• Proud • Confident in me • Relaxed • Pleased	• Parents or caregivers may notice the DOer is using tools and strategies for studying. • The DOer may be understanding the material well because they are learning it in small chunks. • Parents or caregivers may offer positive comments. • The teacher may become aware of needed accommodations for studying.	• Proud • Pleased • Calm • Responsible

Consider this:
How might this map change if the parents or caregivers were not home?

STUDYING AT HOME
(PARENTS OR CAREGIVERS ARE PRESENT)
Behaviors That Are **UNEXPECTED** for the Situation

Behaviors, feelings, and possible actions or reactions are listed in categories in arbitrary order. There is not a one-to-one correlation between the information listed in each column. For example, whatever behavior is listed first does not have to match to the first feeling or action or reaction, and so on.

Unexpected Behaviors for the Situation	How Others Might Feel (or Think)	Possible Actions or Reactions	How the DOer Might Feel (or Think)
• Cramming at the last minute. • Staying quiet when help is needed for study skills. • Ignoring studying for tests. • Cheating rather than studying.	• Confused • Frustrated • Annoyed • Disappointed • Worried	• Poor grade on the test. • Adults may be frustrated that the DOer isn't making time to study. • Negative consequences (failing, expulsion, etc.) for cheating. • Having negative feelings about study skills.	• Disappointed in myself • Stupid • Frustrated

SENDING AND RECEIVING TEXTS AT SCHOOL
Behaviors That Are **EXPECTED** for the Situation

Behaviors, feelings, and possible actions or reactions are listed in categories in arbitrary order. There is not a one-to-one correlation between the information listed in each column. For example, whatever behavior is listed first does not have to match to the first feeling or action or reaction, and so on.

Expected Behaviors for the Situation	How Others Might Feel (or Think)	Possible Actions or Reactions	How the DOer Might Feel (or Think)
• Texting or responding to texts only when it's OK to do so. • Texting someone to express interest in them, say hello, ask about their plans, and see if they may want to hang out. • Texting classmates to find out school-related assignments or information. • Asking a trusted peer or adult about the hidden expectations of sending/receiving texts.	• Calm • Friendly • Happy	• The teacher may notice the DOer follows the rules about phones in school. • People may be friendly because the DOer has shown interest in them. • Classmates might text the DOer to get information about assignment. • Others may initiate or respond to the DOer's texts.	• Happy • Pleased • Accepted • Included

Consider this:
How might this map look different for family members?

SENDING AND RECEIVING TEXTS AT SCHOOL
Behaviors That Are **UNEXPECTED** for the Situation

Behaviors, feelings, and possible actions or reactions are listed in categories in arbitrary order. There is not a one-to-one correlation between the information listed in each column. For example, whatever behavior is listed first does not have to match to the first feeling or action or reaction, and so on.

Unexpected Behaviors for the Situation	How Others Might Feel (or Think)	Possible Actions or Reactions	How the DOer Might Feel (or Think)
• Constantly texting the same person, even if they are not responding. • Sending non-urgent texts in the middle of class. • Sending illegal, violent, or threatening texts. • Ignoring texts that need a reply from classmates, friends, or family. • •	• Confused • Angry • Annoyed • Irritated • Worried → • •	• Others may be annoyed or confused if receiving too many texts. • Others may be irritated if someone is texting while having an in-person conversation. • Others may stop texting or including the DOer if they are ignored. • Law enforcement or security might be notified if threatening texts are sent/received. → • •	• Sad • Stressed • Mad • Excluded • Rejected • •

Copyright © 2023 Think Social Publishing, Inc. All Rights Reserved. From the book, *Social Situation Mapping* by Winner and Crooke. www.socialthinking.com

SAFETY ONLINE AND ON SOCIAL MEDIA
Behaviors That Are **EXPECTED** for the Situation

Behaviors, feelings, and possible actions or reactions are listed in categories in arbitrary order. There is not a one-to-one correlation between the information listed in each column. For example, whatever behavior is listed first does not have to match to the first feeling or action or reaction, and so on.

Expected Behaviors for the Situation	How Others Might Feel (or Think)	Possible Actions or Reactions	How the DOer Might Feel (or Think)
• Only sharing non-personal information (screen name, handle, etc.). • Only sharing photos with family, friends, or friends of friends. • Setting boundaries for how often and when to connect with others online. • Keeping personal details private or only viewable to family and close friends. • Only sharing personal information such as address, phone number, school name, or location with family and close friends. • •	• Trusted • Respectful • Safe • Comfortable • •	• Safety boundaries might be clear to others online. • Others may recognize the DOers information is private. • Parents or caregivers and others may notice the DOer is being safe online. • •	• Calm • Pleased • Happy • Safe • •

SAFETY ONLINE AND ON SOCIAL MEDIA
Behaviors That Are UNEXPECTED for the Situation

Behaviors, feelings, and possible actions or reactions are listed in categories in arbitrary order. There is not a one-to-one correlation between the information listed in each column. For example, whatever behavior is listed first does not have to match to the first feeling or action or reaction, and so on.

Unexpected Behaviors for the Situation	How Others Might Feel (or Think)	Possible Actions or Reactions	How the DOer Might Feel (or Think)
• Sharing private information such as full name, contact information, and location. • Giving out personal details about family members. • Sending sexually explicit pictures or videos to strangers. • Making plans to meet online acquaintance without discussing with trusted adult or parents.	• Confused • Scared • Worried • Exploited • Threatened • Manipulated	• People may try to steal from or cheat the DOer. • Others may use the personal information to steal their identity. • Others may use the pictures or videos inappropriately (repost, share, use to embarrass, etc.). • Personal safety may be at risk.	• Angry • Sad • Scared • Stressed • Vulnerable • Embarrassed

VISITING ANOTHER PERSON'S HOUSE
Behaviors That Are **EXPECTED** for the Situation

Behaviors, feelings, and possible actions or reactions are listed in categories in arbitrary order. There is not a one-to-one correlation between the information listed in each column. For example, whatever behavior is listed first does not have to match to the first feeling or action or reaction, and so on.

Expected Behaviors for the Situation	How Others Might Feel (or Think)	Possible Actions or Reactions	How the DOer Might Feel (or Think)
• Ringing the doorbell or knocking and waiting until someone answers. • Greeting the person who answers. Acknowledging everyone who may be at the house. • Making suggestions but being flexible about what activities to do. • If present, thanking the parents or caregivers before leaving.	• Calm • Friendly • Happy • Safe	• Other people may think the DOer is polite and grateful. • The DOer may enjoy being invited. • Everyone might enjoy hanging out together. • The parents or caregivers may be happy to have DOer come over again in the future.	• Calm • Pleased • Happy • Included

Consider this:
How might this map look different if you were visiting a family member's house?

VISITING ANOTHER PERSON'S HOUSE
Behaviors That Are **UNEXPECTED** for the Situation

Behaviors, feelings, and possible actions or reactions are listed in categories in arbitrary order. There is not a one-to-one correlation between the information listed in each column. For example, whatever behavior is listed first does not have to match to the first feeling or action or reaction, and so on.

Unexpected Behaviors for the Situation	How Others Might Feel (or Think)	Possible Actions or Reactions	How the DOer Might Feel (or Think)
• Walking into a house without knocking or ringing the bell. • Ignoring other people at the house who ask questions or say hello. • Wandering around the house alone. • Insisting on only doing certain activities. • Complaining to the parents or caregivers or refusing to thank them.	• Confused • Annoyed • Upset • Hurt • Mad • Offended	• Others may be confused if the DOer doesn't say hello. • The host may not enjoy the visit. • The parents or caregivers may think the DOer is ungrateful or inconsiderate. • The DOer may not be invited in the future.	• Upset • Sad • Lonely • Stressed • Embarrassed

HAVING VISITORS WHEN ADULTS ARE HOME
Behaviors That Are **EXPECTED** for the Situation

Behaviors, feelings, and possible actions or reactions are listed in categories in arbitrary order. There is not a one-to-one correlation between the information listed in each column. For example, whatever behavior is listed first does not have to match to the first feeling or action or reaction, and so on.

Expected Behaviors for the Situation	How Others Might Feel (or Think)	Possible Actions or Reactions	How the DOer Might Feel (or Think)
• Greeting them at the door. • Introducing them to parents and/or whoever else is home. • Asking them what they would like to do. • Offering them a snack or drink. • If unsure or uncomfortable, asking a trusted family member to coach or help to make the visitor feel welcome.	• Welcome • Friendly • Happy • Safe	• The visitor might feel welcome and want to come back. • The DOer and visitor may figure out they like spending time together. • The parents or caregivers may give everyone space to make their own choices about activities. • The DOer might get practice and become more comfortable hanging out with others.	• Happy • Pleased • Calm • Included

Consider this:
How might this map change when a familiar friend visits when no adults are home?

HAVING VISITORS WHEN ADULTS ARE HOME
Behaviors That Are **UNEXPECTED** for the Situation

Behaviors, feelings, and possible actions or reactions are listed in categories in arbitrary order. There is not a one-to-one correlation between the information listed in each column. For example, whatever behavior is listed first does not have to match to the first feeling or action or reaction, and so on.

Unexpected Behaviors for the Situation	How Others Might Feel (or Think)	Possible Actions or Reactions	How the DOer Might Feel (or Think)
• Ignoring the person at the door. • Leaving the person alone to figure out what to do. • Calling or texting other people. • Refusing to compromise on shared activities.	• Confused • Frustrated • Embarrassed • Hurt • Mad • Offended	• The visitor might feel unwelcome and not want to come back. • The visitor may get bored or want to leave. • The visitor may tell others about their negative experience.	• Sad • Mad • Stressed • Alone • Upset

AT A SCHOOL DANCE
Behaviors That Are **EXPECTED** for the Situation

Behaviors, feelings, and possible actions or reactions are listed in categories in arbitrary order. There is not a one-to-one correlation between the information listed in each column. For example, whatever behavior is listed first does not have to match to the first feeling or action or reaction, and so on.

Expected Behaviors for the Situation	How Others Might Feel (or Think)	Possible Actions or Reactions	How the DOer Might Feel (or Think)
• Hanging out with familiar peers or friends and watching people dance. • Dancing in groups. • Nicely accepting or declining dance requests. • Asking others to dance. • Making related or supportive comments when chatting in groups. • Taking a break from the noise, lights, and movement if needed (and letting chaperones know). • •	• Friendly • Satisfied • Happy • Included → • •	• People may want the DOer to dance (in groups or individually). • People may enjoy chatting or hanging out with the DOer. • Others might see the DOer as friendly, kind, or approachable. • The DOer might feel proud that they tried something that can be both fun and uncomfortable. • The DOer can practice advocating for their own sensory and social needs. → • •	• Happy • Pleased • Calm • Included • •

AT A SCHOOL DANCE
Behaviors That Are UNEXPECTED for the Situation

Behaviors, feelings, and possible actions or reactions are listed in categories in arbitrary order. There is not a one-to-one correlation between the information listed in each column. For example, whatever behavior is listed first does not have to match to the first feeling or action or reaction, and so on.

Unexpected Behaviors for the Situation	How Others Might Feel (or Think)	Possible Actions or Reactions	How the DOer Might Feel (or Think)
• Criticizing people's clothes, how they dance, or other personal characteristics. • Hiding or leaving the dance without letting someone know. • Playing video games. • Asking the same person to dance repeatedly even if they have declined.	• Confused • Irritated • Uncomfortable • Upset • Unfriendly • Offended	• People may avoid the DOer because of their mean comments. • Others may think the DOer is not approachable. • Adults may worry if the DOer disappears, even for a short time.	• Annoyed • Hurt • Sad • Lonely • Upset

FLOSSING AT HOME
Behaviors That Are **EXPECTED** for the Situation

Behaviors, feelings, and possible actions or reactions are listed in categories in arbitrary order. There is not a one-to-one correlation between the information listed in each column. For example, whatever behavior is listed first does not have to match to the first feeling or action or reaction, and so on.

Expected Behaviors for the Situation	How Others Might Feel (or Think)	Possible Actions or Reactions	How the DOer Might Feel (or Think)
• Flossing every day. • Flossing in a bathroom or in private. • Throwing away the floss in the garbage. • Cleaning the mirror if needed.	• Happy • Grateful • Pleased	• Healthy gums and teeth. • Parents or caregivers may stop reminding the DOer. • Parents or caregivers might notice and comment on maturity.	• Good • Clean • Happy

Consider this:
How might this map look different if you needed to floss at school? In the store?

FLOSSING AT HOME
Behaviors That Are **UNEXPECTED** for the Situation

Behaviors, feelings, and possible actions or reactions are listed in categories in arbitrary order. There is not a one-to-one correlation between the information listed in each column. For example, whatever behavior is listed first does not have to match to the first feeling or action or reaction, and so on.

Unexpected Behaviors for the Situation	How Others Might Feel (or Think)	Possible Actions or Reactions	How the DOer Might Feel (or Think)
• Flossing in front of others in shared spaces. • Leaving floss laying around. • Leaving pieces of food on the mirror, sink, or area where flossing.	• Confused • Frustrated • Angry • Disappointed • Surprised	• Unhealthy gums or teeth. • People might get "grossed out" and make negative comments. • Parents or caregivers might make negative or corrective comments.	• Upset • Embarrassed • Anxious • Unhappy

DAILY HYGIENE ROUTINE AT HOME OR WHEN TRAVELING
Behaviors That Are **EXPECTED** for the Situation

Behaviors, feelings, and possible actions or reactions are listed in categories in arbitrary order. There is not a one-to-one correlation between the information listed in each column. For example, whatever behavior is listed first does not have to match to the first feeling or action or reaction, and so on.

Expected Behaviors for the Situation	How Others Might Feel (or Think)	Possible Actions or Reactions	How the DOer Might Feel (or Think)
• Shower or wash face, under arms, and genital area. • Brush teeth. • Apply deodorant. • Wash, rinse, and/or comb or brush hair. • Put on clean or mostly clean clothes. • •	• Pleased • Happy • Grateful • Impressed → • •	• Parents or caregivers may be proud. • Others may notice the DOer looks nice. • Others may appreciate the DOer's self care. → • •	• Proud • Clean • Happy • Relaxed • •

DAILY HYGIENE ROUTINE AT HOME OR WHEN TRAVELING
Behaviors That Are **UNEXPECTED** for the Situation

Behaviors, feelings, and possible actions or reactions are listed in categories in arbitrary order. There is not a one-to-one correlation between the information listed in each column. For example, whatever behavior is listed first does not have to match to the first feeling or action or reaction, and so on.

Unexpected Behaviors for the Situation	How Others Might Feel (or Think)	Possible Actions or Reactions	How the DOer Might Feel (or Think)
• Sleeping in dirty clothes and wearing repeatedly, even when clean clothes are available. • Refusing to wash face, hair, and other body parts that are dirty or smelly. • Putting on clothes that have food stains or dried food.	• Confused • Grossed out • Annoyed • Disgusted • Surprised	• Others might avoid sitting or standing near the DOer. • Others might notice the DOer's poor hygiene. • The nurse or counselor might call the parents or caregivers. • The DOer might develop a rash or other infection due to poor hygiene.	• Upset • Embarrassed • Anxious • Unhappy
•	•	•	•
•	•	•	•

USING A PUBLIC TOILET
Behaviors That Are EXPECTED for the Situation

Behaviors, feelings, and possible actions or reactions are listed in categories in arbitrary order. There is not a one-to-one correlation between the information listed in each column. For example, whatever behavior is listed first does not have to match to the first feeling or action or reaction, and so on.

Expected Behaviors for the Situation	How Others Might Feel (or Think)	Possible Actions or Reactions	How the DOer Might Feel (or Think)
• Covering the seat with a liner or toilet paper. • Flushing, if the flush is not automatic. • Locking the door. • Washing and drying hands afterward.	• Happy • Grateful • Pleased	• Others are usually glad to find a clean restroom. • Others know when a stall is occupied. • Viruses and bacteria are less likely to spread from the bathroom.	• Good • Clean • Happy

Consider this:
How might this map change if using a toilet at a friend or family member's house?

USING A PUBLIC TOILET
Behaviors That Are **UNEXPECTED** for the Situation

Behaviors, feelings, and possible actions or reactions are listed in categories in arbitrary order. There is not a one-to-one correlation between the information listed in each column. For example, whatever behavior is listed first does not have to match to the first feeling or action or reaction, and so on.

Unexpected Behaviors for the Situation	How Others Might Feel (or Think)	Possible Actions or Reactions	How the DOer Might Feel (or Think)
• Leaving urine on or around the seat or on the floor. • Leaving the stall door open when using the toilet. • Leaving the toilet unflushed. • Leaving without washing hands.	• Confused • Frustrated • Anxious • Angry • Stressed	• Others may be upset that the toilet or stall is covered with urine. • People might be embarrassed if seeing the DOer with the door open. • Others might think the DOer isn't clean or doesn't know to wash their hands.	• Upset • Embarrassed • Anxious • Unhappy • Confused

USING THE URINAL IN A PUBLIC BATHROOM
Behaviors That Are EXPECTED for the Situation

Behaviors, feelings, and possible actions or reactions are listed in categories in arbitrary order. There is not a one-to-one correlation between the information listed in each column. For example, whatever behavior is listed first does not have to match to the first feeling or action or reaction, and so on.

Expected Behaviors for the Situation	How Others Might Feel (or Think)	Possible Actions or Reactions	How the DOer Might Feel (or Think)
• If others are there, picking a urinal far away from them (if possible). • Looking straight ahead or down. • Aiming for the bottom of the urinal, drain, or urinal cake. • Zipping up and washing hands when finished.	• Calm • Comfortable • Relieved	• Others will respect privacy. • The urinal will stay clean. • Washed hands will keep germs from spreading.	• Calm • Comfortable • Relieved

USING THE URINAL IN A PUBLIC BATHROOM
Behaviors That Are **UNEXPECTED** for the Situation

Behaviors, feelings, and possible actions or reactions are listed in categories in arbitrary order. There is not a one-to-one correlation between the information listed in each column. For example, whatever behavior is listed first does not have to match to the first feeling or action or reaction, and so on.

Unexpected Behaviors for the Situation	How Others Might Feel (or Think)	Possible Actions or Reactions	How the DOer Might Feel (or Think)
• Picking a urinal next to someone when there are others open. • Talking to others. • Looking towards others who are urinating. • Leaving without washing hands.	• Confused • Frustrated • Anxious • Angry • Stressed	• Others might make negative comments. • Others might be annoyed and make corrective comments. • Others might think the DOer isn't clean or doesn't know to wash their hands.	• Frustrated • Embarrassed • Mad • Uncomfortable

MEALTIME WITH FAMILY
Behaviors That Are **EXPECTED** for the Situation

Behaviors, feelings, and possible actions or reactions are listed in categories in arbitrary order. There is not a one-to-one correlation between the information listed in each column. For example, whatever behavior is listed first does not have to match to the first feeling or action or reaction, and so on.

Expected Behaviors for the Situation	How Others Might Feel (or Think)	Possible Actions or Reactions	How the DOer Might Feel (or Think)
• Leaving enough food for others to have their own serving. • Thanking the cook or person who prepared or arranged for food. • Chewing with mouth closed. • Talking after food is swallowed.	• Calm • Happy • Proud • Confident • Impressed	• Others may notice and make a positive comment about the DOer's manners. • People might feel appreciated. • There will be enough food for everyone to share.	• Proud • Happy • Calm

MEALTIME WITH FAMILY
Behaviors That Are UNEXPECTED for the Situation

Behaviors, feelings, and possible actions or reactions are listed in categories in arbitrary order. There is not a one-to-one correlation between the information listed in each column. For example, whatever behavior is listed first does not have to match to the first feeling or action or reaction, and so on.

Unexpected Behaviors for the Situation	How Others Might Feel (or Think)	Possible Actions or Reactions	How the DOer Might Feel (or Think)
• Chewing with mouth open. • Talking while food is in mouth. • Taking most or all of the food. • Constantly complaining about the meal.	• Confused • Embarrassed • Frustrated • Stressed • Sad • Worried • Concerned	• Parents or caregivers may make negative or corrective statements. • Others may not enjoy eating together. • Others may think the DOer is inconsiderate or rude.	• Frustrated • Tired • Annoyed • Lonely • Uncomfortable

SHARING WITH SIBLINGS AT HOME
Behaviors That Are **EXPECTED** for the Situation

Behaviors, feelings, and possible actions or reactions are listed in categories in arbitrary order. There is not a one-to-one correlation between the information listed in each column. For example, whatever behavior is listed first does not have to match to the first feeling or action or reaction, and so on.

Expected Behaviors for the Situation	How Others Might Feel (or Think)	Possible Actions or Reactions	How the DOer Might Feel (or Think)
• Occasionally agreeing to share items with siblings. • Clearly and kindly stating special rules about using or returning items. • Thanking siblings once they have returned shared items. • •	• Happy • Proud • Relaxed • Calm • Relieved → • •	• Parents may notice and make positive comments about the sharing. • Siblings may also want to share. • Siblings may feel grateful. → • •	• Happy • Proud • Calm • •

SHARING WITH SIBLINGS AT HOME
Behaviors That Are **UNEXPECTED** for the Situation

Behaviors, feelings, and possible actions or reactions are listed in categories in arbitrary order. There is not a one-to-one correlation between the information listed in each column. For example, whatever behavior is listed first does not have to match to the first feeling or action or reaction, and so on.

Unexpected Behaviors for the Situation	How Others Might Feel (or Think)	Possible Actions or Reactions	How the DOer Might Feel (or Think)
• Ignoring sharing requests from siblings. • Always refusing to share toys or items. • Using mean words to reply to sharing requests. • Giving a long or unreasonable list of rules for using the item.	• Confused • Sad • Frustrated • Tense • Hurt • Overwhelmed	• Caregivers or parents may need to intervene and make rules about sharing. • Siblings may have hurt feelings or feel angry if sharing is not reciprocal. • The family may feel tense if siblings are not getting along. • Everyone might end up arguing instead of having fun and playing.	• Frustrated • Tired • Annoyed • Uncomfortable • Tense

DOING CHORES AT HOME
(PARENTS OR CAREGIVERS ARE HOME)
Behaviors That Are **EXPECTED** for the Situation

Behaviors, feelings, and possible actions or reactions are listed in categories in arbitrary order. There is not a one-to-one correlation between the information listed in each column. For example, whatever behavior is listed first does not have to match to the first feeling or action or reaction, and so on.

Expected Behaviors for the Situation	How Others Might Feel (or Think)	Possible Actions or Reactions	How the DOer Might Feel (or Think)
• Doing chores without being reminded. • If reminded, saying "Okay" and getting the chore done right away. • Staying focused on chore until it is complete. • If struggling to remember, asking for a list or other strategy to learn how to start and finish chores completely without constant oversight.	• Happy • Proud • Relaxed • Calm • Relieved	• Parents or caregivers may make positive comments. • The DOer may receive an allowance or extra privileges. • The DOer may have more time to do other things if the chore is done right the first time. • Parents or caregivers may notice and comment on how the DOer is advocating for help.	• Happy • Proud • Calm

Consider this:
How might this map change if parents or caregivers are not home?

DOING CHORES AT HOME
(PARENTS OR CAREGIVERS ARE HOME)
Behaviors That Are **UNEXPECTED** for the Situation

Behaviors, feelings, and possible actions or reactions are listed in categories in arbitrary order. There is not a one-to-one correlation between the information listed in each column. For example, whatever behavior is listed first does not have to match to the first feeling or action or reaction, and so on.

Unexpected Behaviors for the Situation	How Others Might Feel (or Think)	Possible Actions or Reactions	How the DOer Might Feel (or Think)
• Refusing to do any chores. • Saying, "I'll do that later" or "It's not my job." • Starting but not finishing the chore. • Rushing through the chore and not doing a thorough job.	• Confused • Upset • Frustrated • Tense • Hurt • Stressed	• Chores may not get finished and the house will get messy and disorganized. • The DOer may lose allowance or privileges. • Parents may use frustrated or angry reminders to finish the chore correctly.	• Frustrated • Tired • Annoyed • Uncomfortable • Tense

WATCHING TV WITH OTHERS AT HOME
Behaviors That Are **EXPECTED** for the Situation

Behaviors, feelings, and possible actions or reactions are listed in categories in arbitrary order. There is not a one-to-one correlation between the information listed in each column. For example, whatever behavior is listed first does not have to match to the first feeling or action or reaction, and so on.

Expected Behaviors for the Situation	How Others Might Feel (or Think)	Possible Actions or Reactions	How the DOer Might Feel (or Think)
• Listening to others' ideas about what to watch. • Compromising. • Talking during commercials or when the show is paused. • Being flexible when someone else's choice is picked, knowing that everyone will get a turn to choose. • Using strategies or tools to help watch with the group (headphones, movement break away from the screen, fidget, snacks, etc.).	• Happy • Calm • Relaxed	• Everyone can enjoy TV and time together. • Everyone can watch in their own way without interrupting how others watch in their own way. • The DOer can practice flexibility. • Parents or caregivers might make positive comments.	• Relaxed • Happy • Proud

Consider this:
How might this map change if you are watching TV by yourself?

WATCHING TV WITH OTHERS AT HOME
Behaviors That Are **UNEXPECTED** for the Situation

Behaviors, feelings, and possible actions or reactions are listed in categories in arbitrary order. There is not a one-to-one correlation between the information listed in each column. For example, whatever behavior is listed first does not have to match to the first feeling or action or reaction, and so on.

Unexpected Behaviors for the Situation	How Others Might Feel (or Think)	Possible Actions or Reactions	How the DOer Might Feel (or Think)
• Insisting on selecting the show. • Talking when others are trying to listen to the show. • Telling others what will happen next. • Taking the remote from others while they are using it. • •	• Confused • Annoyed • Angry • Frustrated • Upset • Nervous → • •	• Parents or caregivers may turn off the TV and restrict TV time. • Others may not invite the DOer to watch shows the next time. • Others might make negative comments about the DOer's actions. → • •	• Hurt • Annoyed • Rejected • Sad • •

NEEDING HELP WHEN OTHERS ARE BUSY
Behaviors That Are **EXPECTED** for the Situation

Behaviors, feelings, and possible actions or reactions are listed in categories in arbitrary order. There is not a one-to-one correlation between the information listed in each column. For example, whatever behavior is listed first does not have to match to the first feeling or action or reaction, and so on.

Expected Behaviors for the Situation	How Others Might Feel (or Think)	Possible Actions or Reactions	How the DOer Might Feel (or Think)
• Reading others' plans to decide which person might be available to help. • If the person looks busy, asking if they can help when done. • If the person is on the phone or in a meeting, waiting until they are done before talking to them. • Writing a note with the request and leaving it with the person. • •	• Happy • Proud • Relaxed • Calm • Relieved • •	• Others may notice the DOer was patient or considerate. • Others might be able to stop what they are doing to help. • Others might clarify when they are free to help. • •	• Happy • Proud • Calm • •

NEEDING HELP WHEN OTHERS ARE BUSY
Behaviors That Are **UNEXPECTED** for the Situation

Behaviors, feelings, and possible actions or reactions are listed in categories in arbitrary order. There is not a one-to-one correlation between the information listed in each column. For example, whatever behavior is listed first does not have to match to the first feeling or action or reaction, and so on.

Unexpected Behaviors for the Situation	How Others Might Feel (or Think)	Possible Actions or Reactions	How the DOer Might Feel (or Think)
• Tugging or pulling on a person to get their attention. • Yelling a person's name rather than going to them to ask for help. • Interrupting them while they are on a phone call or in a meeting. • Demanding they stop what they are doing to help when it's not an emergency.	• Confused • Frustrated • Annoyed • Stressed	• Parents or caregivers may scold the DOer. • Others may have trouble completing their important tasks and get frustrated. • Parents or caregivers may explain that it's necessary to wait for a little while. • The DOer may not easily get help.	• Frustrated • Annoyed • Sad • Tense • Embarrassed

GETTING READY FOR BED AT HOME
Behaviors That Are **EXPECTED** for the Situation

Behaviors, feelings, and possible actions or reactions are listed in categories in arbitrary order. There is not a one-to-one correlation between the information listed in each column. For example, whatever behavior is listed first does not have to match to the first feeling or action or reaction, and so on.

Expected Behaviors for the Situation	How Others Might Feel (or Think)	Possible Actions or Reactions	How the DOer Might Feel (or Think)
When given a signal (5-minute warning, alarm, verbal reminder) that it's bedtime: • Stopping play, winding down, or putting things away. • Getting a drink or taking a glass of water to room (if allowed) • Brushing and flossing teeth. • Changing into pajamas. • Getting into bed and staying in bed. • •	• Happy • Proud • Relaxed/calm • Relieved • •	• Everyone might get a good night's sleep. • Parents or caregivers may feel proud. • Parents or caregivers might let the DOer stay up later. • •	• Happy • Proud • Energized the next day • •

GETTING READY FOR BED AT HOME
Behaviors That Are **UNEXPECTED** for the Situation

Behaviors, feelings, and possible actions or reactions are listed in categories in arbitrary order. There is not a one-to-one correlation between the information listed in each column. For example, whatever behavior is listed first does not have to match to the first feeling or action or reaction, and so on.

Unexpected Behaviors for the Situation	How Others Might Feel (or Think)	Possible Actions or Reactions	How the DOer Might Feel (or Think)
• Refusing to stop playing video games, with toys, or other activities. • Sleeping in clothes. • Going to bed with dirty teeth or body. • Getting up repeatedly and waking up other family members.	• Confused • Frustrated • Worried • Angry • Stressed • Upset	• People in the house may not get enough sleep and be grumpy the next day. • Parents or caregivers may take away privileges. • People might notice poor hygiene.	• Frustrated • Tired • Annoyed • Uncomfortable

About the Authors

Michelle Garcia Winner, MA, CCC-SLP, is the founder of Social Thinking®, CEO of Think Social Publishing, Inc., and a globally recognized thought leader, author, speaker, and social-cognitive therapist. She is dedicated to helping people of all ages develop social emotional learning, including those with social learning differences. Across her 35+ year career she has created numerous evidence-based and evidence-informed strategies and teaching frameworks. Michelle's work also teaches how social competencies impact overall well-being, including one's ability to foster relationships and their academic and career performance. She and her team continually update the Social Thinking® Methodology based on the latest research and insights they learn from their clients. She was honored to receive a *Congressional Special Recognition Award* in 2008, and a *Lectureship Award* (2019) from the Society of Developmental and Behavioral Pediatricians.

Pamela Crooke, PhD, CCC-SLP, is Chief Curriculum Officer and Director of Research, Content, Clinical Services, and the Social Thinking Training & Speakers' Collaborative at Think Social Publishing, Inc. She served as a clinical faculty member of three universities and worked as a speech-language pathologist in the Arizona public schools for 15 years. Pam is a prolific speaker both in North America and abroad, and has co-authored five award-winning books related to Social Thinking with Michelle Garcia Winner. Their book, *You Are a Social Detective!* 2nd Edition (2020), won the 2021 *Creative Child Magazine* Preferred Choice Award, the 2021 Mom's Choice Gold Medal Award, the 2021 Best Book Awards Finalist, and the 2022 International Book Awards Finalist. They co-authored the companion *You Are a Social Detective! Teaching Curriculum and Support Guide* (2022). She and Michelle collaborate on writing articles and blogs that appear on the Social Thinking website and in a wide array of publications. Her current research focuses on using practice-based research to examine how professionals and parents use frameworks and strategies within the Social Thinking® Methodology.